Berrytales

Plays In One Act

Cheryl E. Davis

Davis, Cheryl E.
     Berrytales.
Cheryl E. Davis ©2001. 268 pp.
     ISBN 1-929229-08-9

1. Reading   2. Education   3. Title

aha! Process, Inc.
(800) 424-9484

Berry is smart
but not smart enough to figure out
all the hidden rules in school
without help.

Berrytales

CHERYL E. DAVIS

Plays you don't expect
about students
and their teachers ...
plays that just might
make you smarter

aha! Process, Inc.
(800) 424-9484

Berrytales
Plays in One Act

Table of Contents

Acknowledgments   **page vii**

Foreword   **page ix**

Author's Tips for Using *Berrytales*:   **page xi**
    An Instructional Framework and Mediation Strategies

The Ghost in the Stories
An Introduction ...   **page 1**
    ... to Berry G, Fonso, Eddie, and Roxy and their alter egos,
    Berry B, Ally, Edy, and Rocky—you figure it out.

Brain in a Box
Part 1   **page 23**
    Four students who would never, ever be friends are
    forced by their Science teacher, Donatelli, to do a project
    together—only they can't find Berry. But they do discover
    his Lizard Brain.

The Lucy Show
Part 2   **page 53**
    Members of the foursome have a semester exam to pass.
    They get all the answers to the exam, and the "in" group,
    led by Lucy, head cheerleader, steals them. Or thinks she does.

You Are Here
Part 3   **page 89**
    Donatelli's Space Unit is, like, getting lost in the mall.
    At least that's how everyone feels, except Berry, who ends
    up losing friends because he breaks rules that he didn't even
    know were there.

aha! Process, Inc.
(800) 424-9484

Third Period
Part 4   **page 129**

As if it's not bad enough that no one's talking to Berry, they all get dumped into an electives class, Drama, that no one wants to take, in a room too small for that many people, and Donatelli gets to teach it because he took a course in Drama once. The good news is … the students co-teach the class, and Berry opts not to take Sewing.

Double Trouble
Part 5   **page 171**

Shakespeare and witches and kings, oh my. They all learn about theater the same way they learn about science. But they get to make more noise and come up with a Readers' Theater version of Macbeth.

Izack, Einstein, and Lady M
Part 6   **page 211**

Gufferson doesn't show up for History. And neither does a sub. No one wants to do the assignment about the Civil War anyway. So, thanks to Berry's group and Officer Larry, the class improvises a meeting of Isaac Newton, Albert Einstein, and Lady Macbeth to discover the causes of the U.S. Civil War.

aha! Process, Inc.
(800) 424-9484

Acknowledgments

Special thanks to ...

MY MOTHER.

MR. FARREL HUMPHREYS, my high school counselor, for finding a way for me to go to college and for refusing to accept that my family couldn't afford it. (And for standing outside Health Class so I couldn't cut class my last semester and keep from graduating.)

DR. NIKKI HANSEN for letting me work my senior year in college doing research on Modern Drama—after I had all the freshman composition papers read.

DR. MARILOU SORENSEN for opening the world of children's literature to me and letting me finish my master's degree by writing a play.

DESSIE TROHALIDES for that first computer and space to write.

OPRAH WINFREY for her example and for a forum to, finally, tell the truth.

TYLER, JESSIE, AND THEIR MOTHER, CONNIE.

ALL THE PEOPLE, ESPECIALLY DR. DEBBIE EMERY AND DR. CHERYL JOHNS, at Truitt Middle School who helped me be the kind of teacher I most want to be.

AND DR. RUBY PAYNE for her love of learning, personally and professionally, and the opportunity to add my heart to her life's work, the elimination of poverty as a reason students (and their teachers) cannot be as successful as they want to be.

aha! Process, Inc.
(800) 424-9484

Foreword

Welcome to *Berrytales*! For years Cheryl Davis and I have had conversations about what learning really means and how to help students learn faster—almost effortlessly. Both of us have been intrigued with the role of story in learning and memory, as well as the need for dialogue in learning.

Berrytales manages to combine dialogue, story narrative, improvisation, and content constructs into plays for students. Specifically, Cheryl has designed these plays for middle school students and their teachers. Each play works easily in the classroom setting. All of the *Berrytales* are about how to teach students science, history, drama, and language constructs—and how to get them to think about their own thinking.

I am very pleased with the results and trust you will be as well. The frontier of taking all students to a much higher level of metacognition is just beginning. It is our hope that *Berrytales* will take us one step farther into that frontier.

Sincerely,
Ruby Payne

aha! Process, Inc.
(800) 424-9484

Berrytales

Author's Tips for Using *Berrytales*

AN INSTRUCTIONAL FRAMEWORK AND MEDIATION STRATEGIES

These plays are written especially for middle school students and their teachers to jump-start and improve cognition in the classroom.

Cognitive learning (and teaching) is like an archeological dig: After the obvious discoveries, it's most successfully done in the worst or least likely situations.

Cognitive learning and archeology are messy and time-consuming. The best tools money can buy don't work as well or as safely as common objects improvised to fit the needs. There's a good chance some thief or graverobber has been there before you without a thought to how important the goods would be as artifacts. Unless you find nothing at all, you often don't know exactly what you have, until later. And then the government of the country it was found in can keep it and not even show it to the public. But regardless of the endings, the stories of the dig will be told over and over again, until others remembering the stories go out and dig for themselves and tell their own stories.

Therefore, before you dig, here are a few of the embedded assumptions and realities of Berrytales.

- Plays are written to be read out loud and acted out in class, as well as performed for an audience.

- Plays, including *Berrytales*, are made to be edited, abridged, and adjusted to fit the needs and circumstances of the players and audience.

aha! Process, Inc.
(800) 424-9484

- Performing the plays and/or scenes from the plays motivates and drives the reading and rereading, thereby increasing concrete to abstract understanding of characters, concepts, and content, with a special focus on Science, English, History, and Theatre Arts.

- These plays are written to share and improve student and teacher knowledge of hidden rules that exist in the use of language and learning behaviors in the frameworks of poverty, middle class, and wealth.

- *Berrytales* are written to model and improve test-taking strategies, learning skills, and casual- to formal-language mediation.

- These plays are written with four primary characters in order to create and model classroom reading/performing teams.

- All primary characters, including teachers' roles, have been given opposite-gender identities and names, in order to secure character/reader identification.

- Team reading and production of plays ensures active student participation and responsibility in the less-threatening framework of small groups.

- Other character traits and background information will be evident as the plays unfold or will be supplied by students as they read, interpret, develop, and perform each play.

- In the Shakespearean sections the playwright is *paraphrased* at a number of points to enhance readability and understanding for 21st-century students.

- In odd-numbered classes, or where otherwise needed (e.g., to back up students with problems in reading/English, mastery, or confidence), two students may share one part.

- Plays have been and can be translated into other languages for and by ESL students to work on and be performed in their own languages as valid optional classwork. This also gives English-only students access to understanding and respect for other students' experiences and languages.

MEDIATION STRATEGIES

(Used to dig out the formal-language knowledge and skills buried in each play.)

Students and/or teachers   alone, in pairs; in teams

List all casual-register words
       by line
       by page
       by scene
       by play

Alphabetize; recopy   alone, in pairs; in teams
       (leave room between
           words)

Define each casual word   alone (separate lists),
       in synonyms or   *then* in pairs
          in synonymous   or teams,
          phrases   add to definitions
          (no inappropriate   (shared words and
          words allowed)   definitions)

List all formal-language words   alone, in pairs; in teams
       by line
       by page
       by scene
       by play

Alphabetize and recopy   (separate lists)

Define each formal word
       in 1-3 words   (shared words and
                                 definitions)

© **aha!** Process, Inc.
(800) 424-9484

Make a T-chart
Code RED for casual
List casual words
      (on **right** side)
Code BLACK for formal
List formal words
      (on **left** side)

alone, in pairs; in teams

Complete T-chart: Find formal for casual and casual for formal.

• **Repeat, substituting "Sentence fragment" for "Casual"**
     and rewriting as complete sentences.
• **Use blank T-chart for practice tests and testing.**
• **Have students compose their own tests and answer keys.**

The neverending Berrytales ...
An Introduction

A Play in One Act
The Ghost in the Stories
Cheryl E. Davis

CHARACTERS

The Boyz	The Girlz	
BERRY B	**BERRY G**	... not cool dressers ... glasses ... computer wizards
EDDIE	**EDY**	... surfer dude, dudette, street or beach
FONSO	**ALLY**	... cool, "the bomb" (not to grown-ups)
ROCKY	**ROXY**	... whatever ... Harley to hip hop ... anything not popular to anyone else, anywhere

THE SETTING

The classroom (the stage) is dark.

Music plays for 80 seconds.

(Samples of four different popular songs are played together. The music is selected by each set of characters, unless they can't agree. Then there could be as many as eight numbers in the mix.)

All characters remain unseen but are positioned across the stage in a wide arc. They are spaced boy-girl but not by character partners, so that each pair is separated. Each has a flashlight (unless there happen to be spots for each one).

At first each character will walk to the middle, downstage center, before speaking and flip the flashlight on, pointed from just below the chin at the face. The light is turned on just before the character speaks.

aha! Process, Inc.
(800) 424-9484

The boyz and the girlz all have their walk and their talk going as they enter. The beat and the rap are whatever each actor wants to do—and can do—together.

BERRY B	Once upon a space …
EDDIE	In a time, like an awesome wine-
FONSO	-ding WAVE … around the block, and down the bend … in the street
BERRY B	There lived four friends.
FONSO	At school … who rule.
ROCKY	Whatever!
ROXY	I say, Whatever!

Snaps her fingers, north and south and east.

That is what I say to be, to be, cool.

ROCKY	And I stay, yes, I stay that way: cool. My one rule. And no one …
ROXY & ROCKY	We say, No one … Ru-u-ules our coo-ool!
BERRY G	Once upon a rhyme … upon the time
ALLY	That it takes to bust a beat
EDY	On the street with our feet,

EDDIE	Hangin' out … on the o-ver-tow.
EDY & EDDIE	Turn. Slam. Zippity bam. We jam!
ROXY	Whatever!
ROCKY	What, she said. Whatever!
FONSO	Name's a game … being the main …
ALLY	Same. Mind. Soul. Good to go.
FONSO & ALLY	You GO, Girl! You go, Boy! GO!

All lights on.

ALL	HEL-LO! We say, Hello.

All lights off.

Changing the pace.

BERRY B *To the audience.*	I'm Berry B. Just call me Berry. Excuse me. If I try to do this rap any longer I will personally be so embarrassed that I'll—
BERRY G	Have to disappear.
BERRY B	I'm not good at rap. I'm not sure I even like it.
BERRY G	I like it. Some of it. But I'm not good at it either. I have a hard time with the beat and talking fast.
BERRY B	There's really only one of us.
BERRY G	That's all you'll see in the plays about us.

BERRY B   After this one.

BERRY G   And Berry B is what you'll see, not me.

BERRY B   Me.

BERRY G   But I'm there. In the lines. Even though his voice does the talking. All you have to do is fix the pronouns so they agree with me as a girl.

BERRY B   We are different points of a similar view.

BERRY G   But we know some people just can't get into a part—

BERRY B   A role—

BERRY G   Thank you.

BERRY B   No. Thank **you.**

BERRY G   If as a girl, you have to play a boy.

BERRY B   Or boyz have to read the girlz' parts.

They step back.
Lights off. Really fast
and making sounds
even before they start. **We** wanted you to **see** how **ea**sy it would **be**—

From the darkness.   Stop that, now!

They look a lot alike.
EDDIE   Sorry. Rhymin's real easy for me—

EDY   —Too.
Points her flashlight. I mean for me too.
at Eddie, then they But you'll just hear Eddie say the lines in the
point the light at her. "Tales" after this. It's just like with the Berry duu-uude.

aha! Process, Inc.
(800) 424-9484

EDDIE	Du-ude, it's OK.
EDY	Du-u-dette to you!
EDDIE *They high-five,* *awkwardly juggling* *the flashlights.*	All right! Just change the names. From mine to hers. Underneath all the differences our characters share the same feelings.
To audience.	Oh. Her name is like my initials—E.D.
EDY	Other characters (well, I mean their actors) will have to fix the pronouns for me—from "he" to "she" and "his" to "hers." You know, no big deal.
EDDIE	We just wanted to make sure you had some choices.
EDY	All right. Thanks, duu-uude. Cool shoes.
EDDIE	Check it out; I was just going to say that about yours. Love your sweater.
EDY	Hilfiger.
EDDIE *Their lights off.*	Like mine. Coo-ool.
Light on. **FONSO**	'Sup?
Both lights on. **ALLY**	You're now looking at Fonso. 'Sup?
FONSO *They go through* *some hand-slapping* *finger pops and start* *to hug, then **freeze.***	And my alter ego, the Lady AL-LEE! Check it out!

*They both point at
each other.*

ALLY	Pass. A'ight.
FONSO	I—
ALLY	We—
FONSO	My bad. We—however you decide to break it down—don' exactly talk like this at school, in class, OK …
ALLY	In front of our friends. Or any of our three thousand cousins.
FONSO	Not Berry … or Eddie … or Roxy. Our friends from the neighbor—
ALLY	—The Hood. Not school. Not Berry or Edy or Rocky. They're different. And not everybody understands that. Even them.
FONSO	But there is a BIG difference.
ALLY	That's just one thing Fonso and I have in common.
FONSO	See—all the stories we ever heard about.
ALLY	In books and in the streets, in the 'Plex …
FONSO	The stories all have characters, and if you really like one, then you're stuck if it's a girl, 'coz then they CAN'T be like you. And you sure CAN'T be like them. That's just how it is.
ALLY	There's a lot of rules like that. Go figure who made 'em up. And you don't always know where all the rules are until—

FONSO	—You mess up.
ALLY	Then you hear about it. And not all quiet-like either.
FONSO	Teachers and schools have the most messed-up rules too.
ALLY	Except for Berry. He has rules for everything. Which is another story I'll get back to. Anyways—
FONSO	What's true for you?
ALLY	What keeps you cool with your family or your friends or just the people walking through? Will—
FONSO	Let me empha-size that ... What's cool for you **will definitely** create heat at school. And teachers do not hold back. It's like their **job** to let you know you broke a rule. Even if you really like the teacher.
ALLY	Like Donatelli. He has GOT to tell you when you break a rule.
FONSO	About school.
ALLY	He usually won't do it in front of the entire universe though.
FONSO	Worse. He'll cover for you.
ALLY	Front it right with your friends, like I'm in trouble and have to stay after school or get lifetime detention watching the Golf Channel.
FONSO	You get there, and the dude's all happy to see you and puts you in charge of a study group, so you have to get an **A,** which he will keep anyone from knowing about—if you get one.

ALLY	Which is cool. He knows I don' want some little punk monkey telling my business all over the place, 'specially if it's going to make my friends and my family think I've sold them out.
FONSO	Become like the MAN.
ALLY	Or the WO-man.

They high-five each other.

FONSO	Just remember, we both dress right.
ALLY	Whatever is cool, we are hooked up.
FONSO	And there isn't a sport we aren't the baddest in.
ALLY	Check it out.
FONSO	And Berry ... for all the brain—
ALLY	Does not have a clue ...
FONSO	About cool. And Eddie—
ALLY	Edy.
FONSO	Her too. They have style. All their own. And if you're down
ALLY	And you just want to hang out
FONSO	And need a laugh and a friend, in comes the board du-ude.
ALLY	Du-u-dette!
FONSO	Who I used to think was just one big worthless flake.

Lights out.

aha! Process, Inc.
(800) 424-9484

Lights on both Roxy and Rocky. There is a very "leather" look here, so that the following lines are totally unexpected and not entirely understood (though the anger and emotion are real).

Dramatically.

ROXY   Once upon a time. No joke. This room. This place. This school. Wasn't. Isn't. It was an illusion. It only existed in someone else's mind. Someone else's head.

Pause.

A little red schoolhouse on the prairie. In the woods. By the river. In the upstairs apartment in the crowded tenement across from the Statue of Liberty. In the orphanages behind Michigan Avenue after the Big Fire. In the missions of Los Angeles and Santa Cruz and Albuquerque.

Pause.

And whoever remembers, thinks the memory is school. Back in the day that was better than today.

ROCKY   Like the children were all blond and blue-eyed and peachy-creamy. With lace caps and white collars and farm faces.
And the children, the people, all got along.
Even the bullies.

ROXY   In one freakin' schoolroom. With a big wood or coal stove or a big fan strapped and pulled, flappin' the air around. Everyone got along.
In the old days.

ROCKY   Back in the days when you studied "The Basics" …

ROXY
Sarcastically.

The Three R's. Readin', 'Ritin', 'Rithmetic. And they say we can't spell. And they did it on—

ROCKY

—Hard wooden desks nailed together on rails that never went anywhere.

ROXY

And you worked school **in,** after chores …

ROCKY

Unless you were rich, then the teacher came to your house until you went to college.

ROXY

The rest of the students worked it in—if they were allowed—

ROCKY

After the harvest. Or after the planting.
Or after the herd was moved to another field.
Or after the milking was done.

ROXY

And later, after Civil Rights. And after Cesar Chavez.

ROCKY

Now the Great American Dream has put us all in schools. All together in school. Not a place like that, back in the old days.

ROXY

More and more. Bigger and bigger. And summer's still off whether it makes sense or not. Unless you're trying to make up credits or get more credits to get out sooner or play on the team when school starts again.

*All the flashlights
come on, move toward
Roxy and Rocky and
then by the crazy
movement of the lights,
there is a struggle.
All the lights go off,
and just Berry B's
comes on his face.*

3 1833 04234 8109

aha! Process, Inc.
(800) 424-9484

*There are still sounds
of struggling.*

BERRY B Due to technical difficulties the following presentation has been—

Joins in.

EDDIE Like, edited … so that

*Scuffle and struggle
get louder.* Roxy

BERRY B And Rocky …

EDDIE Not the squirrel—I love to say that.

BERRY B The Roxy characters can start all over again and stick to the script a-a-and …

*Grabbing Berry's
flashlight, putting
him in a headlock.*

ROXY Listen, Mr. "Brain in a Box," I thought we were free here!

BERRY B I-I-I only meant … the rules … We de-de-de-

ROXY -cided.

BERRY B Thank you. That … that …

EDDIE That we'd come out here in, like, a very mature way …

*She puts a headlock
on Eddie and Berry.
Rocky holds the
flashlight on her.
The others just stand
around for a moment.* And introduce ourselves and each other, so anyone reading our character would know how we wanted the plays to be. And how they can mess with a play so it works better for them.

ROXY	I thought we **were** improvising.
BERRY B	Improvising what?
ROXY	Whatever.
EDDIE	No, enquiring minds want to know ... trust me. What the heck were you and your shadow, Rocky Balboa, pretending to be? And what the heck were you talking about?
BERRY B	She was representing the voice, the outrage of the students of America.
ROCKY	In the **world,** man!

Everyone steps forward, and the house lights come on.

FONSO	She—
ALLY	He.
EDY	They.
FONSO	OK, **they** were just acting like Big Shots so "they" could show off "their," **her,** great big vocabulary and DRAMA talent!
ROXY	Whatever.
ROCKY	I have a big vocabulary too.
ALL	We know.
BERRY G	It gets confusing when both sexes of each character are all on stage together.
EDDIE	You can't say "sex."

Everyone laughs.

BERRY B	OK, "gender."
EDY	What in the heck's a "gender"?
ROXY	Gender means whether you're a boy or a girl.

Eddie/Edy continue
not *to understand.*

To Eddie.

ROCKY	Your character is one of the boyz.

Then to Edy.   And her character is one of the girlz. Dig?

EDDIE	Oh … **oh**! And our character is **EDDIE** in all the stories.
EDY	Unless they can't hack that. Then they can replace you with me. Like there are replacements for everyone, if they want.
EDDIE & EDY	Ooo-kay!
EDDIE	I knew that.

Skeptically.

EDY	Really …
ALL	Uh-huh. You knew that.
FONSO	What we still do **not** know is what Roxy and Bo Bo were talking about.
ALLY	They were getting carried away. It's a **play.** C'mon. Once you get over all the embarrassment, being in a play is a real trip.

Everyone agrees
loudly for a moment.
To Roxy/Rocky.

FONSO	And you were both … TRIPPIN' … large.

ROXY   We liked doing that better than:

She walks downstage
a little and acts
very mechanical.

"Hello. Just in case you have never been in or directed a play before and don't have a clue, you can practically rearrange everything in a play, as long as it works. Please let me explain some facts to you."

FONSO   Get off the robot and do your parts like you're supposed to.

ALLY   You didn't have a clue that you could change a scene, move it to the present or the past, switch a character from a boy to a girl if you didn't have enough boys … until Donatelli—

FONSO   —'Splained it to us in Third Period that time.

ROXY &
ROCKY   WHATEVER!

ROXY   Except you and the "Ghost of Fonso Present" there, Miss ALL-LEE, around-the-block girl, just explained it.

EDDIE
& EDY   OK! Our work here is finished.

High-fives.

BERRY B   Word.

BERRY G   You have no idea what that really means.

BERRY B	Yes I do.
BERRY G	Do not. Or I would know.
BERRY B	You can still say it.
BERRY B & G	Then, WORD UP!
ROXY	Do you two have a fever?
ROCKY	A concussion.
ROXY & ROCKY	Whatever!
ALLY	I liked the part about "ghosts." It was a better explanation.

Everyone turns and stares at her, then at Fonso, who shrugs, then suddenly gets it.

FONSO	I know what you're talking about. When Roxy called you the "Ghost of Fonso Present."
EDDIE	I just hit a crack in the pavement, and I'm …
EDY	Spinning in slow motion as I crash into the brick wall …
EDDIE	Or the brick street by the fish market.
ROXY	I don't get it either.

She puts her hand over Rocky's mouth.   And we know. You don't either.

BERRY G	We are like each other's

BERRY B	Ghost. Whoever is speaking …
BERRY G	Saying the lines …
BERRY B	Telling the stories …
BERRY G	Has the ghost of the other
BERRY B	Close by.
EDDIE	For …
EDY	Real?
ROXY & ROCKY *Bopping Eddie and Edy on the head.*	No. In your imagination.
FONSO	In how you think about the characters and the stories.
EDDIE	I knew that.
EDY	Huh-**uh.**
BERRY B	And all the actors and the readers and the audience and the listeners and the author and the director and the crew (if you have one) … all act like ghosts to each character.
ROXY	Whatever experience is real for you, the other possibilities are close by …
FONSO	In your head—
ROXY	—Imagination.
BERRY B	In your thinking.

aha! Process, Inc.
(800) 424-9484

EDDIE	So every story is a ghost story.
Bopping each other. **EDY**	Sh-h-h … no-o. That's not what ghost story means.
ALLY	I like using it though. The idea that every story is full of ghosts.
ROXY *Rocky slowly exits.*	Other ways to see the characters.
EDDIE *Edy slowly exits.*	Other ways to say the lines.
BERRY B *So does the other Berry.*	Other meanings to the words.
FONSO	Other scenes and actions you can put in.
ALLY *She quietly, almost invisibly, exits.* *The rest haul a table and chairs stage center and pretend they are eating at Mickey Dee's.*	Or take out.
EDDIE *Frowning.*	Like how Berry is smart. It's not a cut. It's just that he sees all the things—or a lot more things than I do—about everything. Especially when he's reading. He sees a whole 'nother story behind each word.
BERRY B	So do you sometimes.
FONSO	Like how Roxy can just SEE all the feeling in the lines—when she wants to.

EDDIE	And isn't afraid to BE the character and STAY in character no matter how much I try to get her to laugh.

Silence.

BERRY B	Do you think we need to say anything else about the characters?
EDDIE	Or school?
FONSO	Or about how to read a play?
ROXY	NO! Good grief, the audience isn't stupid. Oh—except how to read a play.

They pick up scripts. And look for a moment.

	You know. All the words on the left side of the page …
BERRY B	In italics.
EDDIE	Slanted lines.
FONSO	Are information.
BERRY B	Directions. Stage directions …
FONSO	… About the set or the actions or the feelings or the lights or something.
EDDIE	And after the first time, you don't even have to read that part, just your lines.
ROXY	The characters' names are in ALL CAPS—
BERRY B	ALL CAPITAL LETTERS.
ROXY	Indented right of the …

BERRY	Italics.
ROXY	**The stage directions!**
EDDIE	You assign parts before you start to read, so the name is something you never read.

Sarcastically.
ROXY	Unless you don't have anything else to do.

Bops Eddie.

Can I finish now? And the lines—

ROXY, BERRY B, & EDDIE	THE DIALOGUE!

Glare at each other.

FONSO	—The actual words each character says are on the right-hand side of the page. It doesn't look like a story. There aren't paragraphs. It was tricky for me at first.
EDDIE	Only you can't tell anyone it was hard for Fonso …

Running away from Fonso who tries to grab him.

… or you will be in very big trouble.

ROXY	We need to explain about reading it more than one time.
EDDIE	Read it more than once. A lot more. Actually you can memorize it this way, without even knowing what you're doing.
BERRY B	He means more than 20 times, making it better …
FONSO	Louder and louder and, like, give the characters really cool voices each time.

EDDIE	Weird voices, man. Get into it. Make up stuff—
ROXY	Stage business …
BERRY B	That a person, your character, would really do.
FONSO	You can pantomime it. Worry about actual props later—pretend you got a Coke—
EDDIE	Or a cigarette.

They all bop him.

ALL	No cigarettes!
ROXY	No smoking, "pretend" or otherwise: WE ARE NOT THE SHEEP OF THE TOBACCO INDUSTRY.
FONSO	See how Roxy gets into character? Pretend you're feeling like that, as you say the words. It's a kick.
EDDIE	It makes reading a play very **ex**-cel-lent!
ROXY	And if you don't like the plays in English …
FONSO	Translate 'em. Put the lines into your own language.
BERRY B	Or just add an accent.
ROXY	I am very cool in Spanish. In fact, an all-girl cast translated us in Third Period. We had so much attitude the security officer came in one time during a performance to see if there was a fight going on.

EDDIE	Donatelli gave this one guy who knew Vietnamese and English like big-time credit for putting "Brain in a Box" in Vietnamese. And performing it for our class.
BERRY B	He means Quon and a couple of guys who didn't speak any English yet.
FONSO	And made all the characters guys.
EDDIE	And I got to read "me" in Vietnamese.
BERRY B	Yup, Quon wrote all the words as sounds for Eddie. And Eddie just added stuff, like "Totally" and "Coo-ool."
EDDIE	"Totally" and "cool" are, like, in every language. And they got rid of Roxy—for a while.
High-fives Roxy, who hits him.	Ouch!
ROXY	I just wish *Berrytales* wasn't such a corny title.
BERRY B	I like it. A tale is a story you keep adding on to and retelling.
EDDIE	Like vampires. Or aliens.
ROXY	OK, but *Berrytales* sounds so … so juvenile.
FONSO	You can just pretend it's for your sister.
BERRY B	Not **my** sister.
EDDIE	Besides, Berry started it. They're his stories.
Silence. *As an ad-lib.*	His TAIL. Hee-haw!
ALL *Starting to exit.*	OK! Finished here.

ROXY	We get better every time.
BERRY B	The "ghost in every story" was our best definition yet.
ROXY	I think it makes a great metaphor for thinking too.
FONSO	Chill before your heads explode. What's a metaphor?
BERRY B	If you had Corona-Daniels for English you'd already **know** what *metaphor* means.
FONSO	I do have him.
EDDIE	Him? Her! You need to go to class more often.
ROXY	Whatever.

The girlz and the boyz walk their walk and exit as the music from the very beginning comes back up.

Blackout.

... And then the music fades.

aha! Process, Inc.
(800) 424-9484

The neverending Berrytales ...
Part 1

A Play in One Act
Brain in a Box

Cheryl E. Davis

CHARACTERS

Students in the same Science Class. If they don't pass this class, they can't graduate.

BERRY G
BERRY B   ... not a cool dresser ... but a **brain**

EDDIE   ... Valley dude or dudette ... board/blade
EDY   extreme ... always has a backpack

FONSO   ... "the bomb" (to kids, not parents or teachers)
ALLY   ... lots of jewelry ... maybe an accent

ROXY   ... whatever
ROCKY

MR. DONATELLI ... Science teacher often referred to as
                  Dr. Don't ... even if he/she never appears,
                  we frequently see or hear evidence of this
                  character

NOTE: Remember when you are reading the play you have to decide which gender and sometimes which name to use for each character. There are really only four main characters, but there are eight names, so you can choose which you want to use.

aha! Process, Inc.
(800) 424-9484

THE SETTING

Backyard of a school. It's a rainy, late afternoon or early evening.

A big, metal double door with glowing light from dirty glass windows dominates upstage—the back of the stage.

Boxes are everywhere. Big ones. Flattened ones. Little ones leaking Styrofoam packing materials. Stacks of newspapers, tied in bundles and loosely spread about the stage, are everywhere. There are garbage cans; maybe a Dumpster; raggedy, weather-beaten brick walls; and chain-link fences.

VOICES	Berry! Berr-rry?
Curtains are tied back.	
A little light comes	
from the door.	
Stage stays quite dark.	
A school bell rings.	
Momentary silence.	
From the silence,	
loudly, but far away …	
VOICE	Berry!!!!????
Two voices can	
be heard. Each is	
getting closer.	
SECOND &	
FIRST VOICES	Berries!!!
From either side	
of the stage.	Berry! We know you're here.
A large box—down, front,	
and right—hops away	
from each voice each time.	
BOTH VOICES	Berry! We know you're out here.
Box just barely hops	
left and right and back	
to its first place.	

aha! Process, Inc.
(800) 424-9484

Yelling.

EDDIE   Ber—aahhhh! Oh, no-oo!

*Crawling from under a fence, hooking a sweater on it. Pulls the string torn loose by the fence. Each time he yells, the box **shakes** and/or **hops** slightly.*

Ma-annn!! I'm blaming you for this, Berry! You owe me a brand-new Tommy Hilfiger genuine soccer shirt. This was no knockoff. Ma-ann! You owe me!

ROXY   I owe you what?

Coming out from the opposite side.

EDDIE   Not you.

In a bigger voice.   Berry owes me a shirt!

ROXY   What are you talking about?

Eddie shows her the shirt tear and string.

Whatever!

Box shakes and jumps.

Berry?
Berry, we need you. Like, totally come out, come out, wherever you are!

Searching.

Then coming back to Eddie, tying up the loose string of Eddie's shirt and putting his hat on her head.

EDDIE	Hey!!
Roxy throws a martial-arts move at Eddie.	OK, OK. Quit it! Berry, we're NOT leaving until we find you. I have to get a passing grade on this project, or I'll flunk the class.
ROXY	AGAIN!
Pulls make-up mirror from pack, adjusting hat and hair.	
EDDIE	Thank you. Flunk it **again.** Berry, you're the only one who knows what we're doing. Donatelli gave us one last chance. O-N-E! ONE!
Box shakes again. Long pause.	Berr-eee!!!!
ROXY	Maybe we should just forget it!
Looking behind her in the mirror. Goes to Eddie, shows him ... what she sees. Keeps talking to Eddie like he was farther away.	Berry is too chicken to help us make our Science presentation the great report it is ... just because he's so scared to give a teeny, tiny little report in Science.
	... And what does Berry care ... just because ...
Makes chicken sounds. Pointing and directing, sneaking up on the box.	
Getting angrier ...	HE can still pass Science ... because HE has a 99 percent test average ... and HE is Donatelli's favorite student OF ALL TIME!

During this, both creep around until they are on either side of the box that moves away.

Imitating the teacher.
EDDIE   "The smartest student in Science I have ever had. Genius!"

Jumps on box.

Muffled but angry.
BOX   Hey!

ROXY   Look, Eddie, a talking box.
Kicks at box while circling it.   Maybe the box will tell us where Berry is.

Pause.

      I said …

Pushing and bumping Eddie off the box.   Maybe the box will tell us how to find **Berry**!

Pause.

With a squished voice.
BOX   I don't think so.

Eddie and Roxy wrestle the box open, trying unsuccessfully to pry Berry out. When they get him out, he jumps back in, making it even harder to pull him up or out. Finally, they stand the box up, with Berry in it.

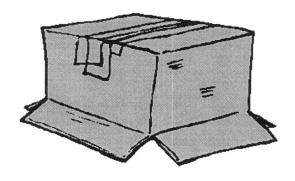

aha! Process, Inc.
(800) 424-9484

They all stand awkwardly, staring at each other.

ROXY   So?

EDDIE   So!

BERRY   So what?
Tries to hop away in box.

ROXY   I don't think so, Boxy Boy.
Holds the top of the box so it can't move.

BERRY   Stop it!
Roxy lets go.
The box falls down.
Moaning.   Ow-w-w!

ROXY   Uh-oh. Get him up.

EDDIE   Ahhgghh. Berry, let go of the box!

BERRY   No-oo!

After a lot of effort and wrestling, Roxy punches a hole in the top of the box as Eddie sits on it. Berry's head sticks out of the hole. Berry stops moaning as soon as his head pops through.

EDDIE   Now **you** are going to stop running away!

aha! Process, Inc.
(800) 424-9484

They all take turns just looking at each other.

BERRY	You can do whatever you want. I don't care. It won't matter. I can't do the report. There's no way I'm going to stand up in front of that class and give a speech about, about—
EDDIE *Reads from his arm.*	Dine-o-SOURs' …
ROXY	… Brains.
EDDIE	Dinosaur brains!
ROXY	Whatever.
BERRY	Anything. I can't give a speech about anything.
ROXY	It's not a speech. It's like a play.
EDDIE	You just have to say your part.
BERRY	It's the same thing. I can't talk in front of people. I turn into a zombie.
ROXY *Joining in.*	You mean a—
EDDIE	Box!

They give each other high-fives.

BERRY *Moaning again.* *He falls into the box.*	Box … zombie. Trust me, it's pretty much the same thing. I'm useless!

*Eddie fishes around
and pulls Berry up.
Berry keeps talking,
even when he's in
the box.*

Hopelessly useless.

I can't even walk.

EDDIE   Man, you walk all the time.

BERRY   Not in front of people.

ROXY   And you **talk** all the **time.**
                   Man, you never shut **up.**

EDDIE   Especially about science. We have to shut you
                   up. Frogs, birds, trees, flowers.

ROXY   Rocks. You even talk about rocks like they're
                   your friends.

BERRY   They are. Rocks tell the history of the world.
*Suddenly speaking
with energy and
enthusiasm. Getting
wilder, like a tent
preacher.*

                   Each line of sediment on a bluff above a river
                   ... each stone holds the moment of time, the
                   heat, the weather, the molecules that happened
                   to it when it was formed.

ROXY   Go, Berry! Go, Berry!
*Eddie joins her in a
little dance.*

EDDIE   See. There you go. Right off the top of your
                   head. That's why Mr. Donatelli put you in our
                   group. You know science, man.

BERRY   What do you mean, put me in your group?
                   It was arbitrary. Chance! An accident.

Sarcastically.

ROXY Like the three worst students in the universe accidentally get put onto a team with "The Brain of the School"? Right!

BERRY OK, OK. It wasn't chance.

You were my **last** chance. Mr. Donatelli said I couldn't write another paper or take a test for this ... I had to do a group presentation or take a **C.**

EDDIE &
ROXY C??

EDDIE **C**? We could get a **C**? Why didn't Dr. Don't tell ME that? I'm getting a **C**! My mom will faint. AND I can get out of being grounded for the rest of the year!

ROXY Wait a minute, Eddie. Eddie!
Chill o-o-out!

To Berry. **Don't-tell-ME** promised you a C?

BERRY Not exactly.
And don't call Mr. Donatelli that.

Imitating Donatelli
and Donatelli's list
of do's and don't's.

EDDIE Don't tell ME!! Don't tell ME!! Don't tell ME!! Dr. Don't: Don't be late! Don't forget your book! Don't talk. Don't daydream. Don't sleep in class. Don't go out with your friends when you have a test to study for!!

Joining in ...

ROCKY Don't tell ME your dog ate your homework! Don't tell ME you want to work at McDonald's the rest of your life. Don't tell ME science isn't fun!

FONSO'S
VOICE
Booming out! Did he promise you a **C** or not?!

Eddie and Roxy greet
Fonso. Berry starts
to hop offstage but
hops right into Fonso. What's up, Little Duck?

The box tries to
retreat. Did he promise you a **C**?

Berry comes out
of the box, nodding.

      BERRY Not exactly. Yes. I mean … no.
Fonso holds Berry's
head still. Maybe. He didn't exactly say that, but he
meant there was no way I'd get an **A** this
semester … if … if I didn't do a report. I wish
you'd let me get back in the box.

Berry scrambles back
into the box. Eddie
sits on the box.

To Fonso.
      EDDIE What are **you** doing here?

      FONSO We need to practice.

      EDDIE Yeah, but … but … you **never** …
Awkward pause. Ah … I didn't think …

      ROXY What Eddie means is … Heck, Fonso, you've
been on our team all year and not once did you
… you never did …

      EDDIE … Even come to a meeting.

      FONSO I had something else … football. It's over now.

From the box.

BERRY   It's the middle of basketball season.

Eddie kicks the box, trying to keep Berry from getting into trouble.

Football's been over since FOREVER ... Everybody knows that.

FONSO   Look. Does anybody have a problem with me being here?

ALL   No. No way. Not me.

FONSO   OK. So ... let's get something done here. What's our topic?

Turns Berry and the box around.

OK, Pinky and Brainiac, 'splain it to me.

*Berry just stands there, frozen, except his mouth is opening and closing, like he's talking, **but** no words come out.*

To Fonso.

EDDIE   Don't watch him.

FONSO   What?

ROXY   Don't look at him. He freaks out ... does this zombie thing. Really!

She turns the box around, so Berry speaks from the box.

BERRY

Fonso turns Berry (AKA the Box) and follows Berry during this speech ... Berry stops talking when he faces out and continues when he is facing away from everyone.

We were assigned to discuss and explain to the class about the origin and significance of the Human Brain Stem.

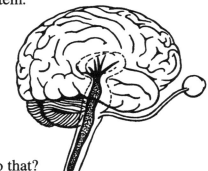

FONSO   How does he do that?

ROXY   Not HOW, but why.

EDDIE   Say it in English, Berry.

BERRY   I did say it in ENGLISH, you ...

They turn the box in. Then out.   (Says nothing ...)

                                        IDIOT!

Fonso turns the box back.   I was talking to Eddie, honest. (Nothing, again ...)

Roxy turns the box away.   I said, The topic we were assigned IS the BRAIN STEM.
You know, how it works and stuff.

ROXY   OK, OK. So our topic is about the brain.
We can do a report on that, easy.

EDDIE   And get a C?

ROXY   Easy. We all got a BRAIN. This'll be a piece of cake. We'll copy some stuff off the Internet, divide it up, and read it ... in class.
So-oo coo-ool.

aha! Process, Inc.
(800) 424-9484

BERRY *Goes back in and out of the box.*	Brain **STEM. The Brain STEM!!!**
EDDIE	Look, Boxy, flowers have stems. Not people.
FONSO	I never heard anything about a stem in our heads.
ROXY	Now you've totally freaked Berry out. We'll ignore him. Who's got a computer?
EDDIE	My stepdad.
FONSO	One of my cousins, if he hasn't sold it yet.
ROXY	Are you, any of you, on-line?
EDDIE *Hopefully.* *Then not.*	Worldwide. Except my dad made it so you can't get any X-rated stuff. But brain ... that's not X. Is it?
ROXY	No, Eddie. Now this is COOL! All we have to do is find some stuff like where the brain is ... and what would happen without one and who has the best ones ...
EDDIE	And who invented them.
ROXY *Bops him!*	Duh!
EDDIE	My bad. Well, who did?
FONSO	We come with one. All animals have one.
EDDIE	Fish too?

ROXY	And birds ... and snakes and turtles and frogs. I know. Once I had to dissect a frog. Well, **I** didn't, but the girl next to me did. My mother sent me to this charter school for gifted kids, so I could find my gift ... whatever ... Anyway, if you jab the brain or the muscles with a battery-charger thing,

She demonstrates with her hands.

the frog moves. Only it's really dead, but ... it gets all overcharged and moves anyway.

FONSO	You saw the brain?
ROXY	Yes. I peeked. It kinda looked like a lima bean.
EDDIE	Did it have a stem?
ROXY	No-oo!
EDDIE	No petals either, I bet.

As the three of them laugh over this, the box turns halfway back toward the audience.

BERRY	"Stem" doesn't have to mean just exactly like a flower has a stem.

The three want to hear Berry. But when they move so they can see him, he turns away from them. By the end of this speech, they have all gone in a big circle around Berry and the box.

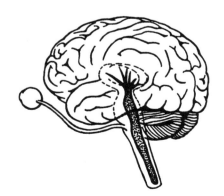

BERRY	The Brain Stem is like a little brain inside a bigger one. Except that most animals' brains are really only like our stem part.
EDDIE	Like a little guy riding on your handlebars?
BERRY	More like a guy riding on your back, who helps you pump and steer. The Brain Stem is the control center for everything in the brain and in us. And it sits in the center and the back of the brain and connects to the spinal cord right at that dent place in the back of your head. You know, right where the neck goes into the head.

Everyone checks.
They all touch
Berry's head.

Hey, that's enough. Anyway, the Brain Stem can't talk. The real part of your brain, the Cerebral Cortex, controls that. The stem does the automatic stuff—breathe, sweat, grow, get hungry. It's an emergency control center. All messages from all our senses go through here and get sent on. It checks everything—looks for danger. That's its No. 1 job: keeping us out of danger. It signals whether we should run or fight.

FONSO	Well, Brain Stem is a pretty wimpy name for it then.
BERRY	It has another name. It's called the Reptilian Brain.
ROXY	**Snake** brain??!
BERRY	More like T-Rex Brain.
EDDIE	Cool!

BERRY	Like I said, it's the part of the human brain most like the brain in other mammals: the lima bean in Roxy's frog—and in fish, amphibians—
EDDIE	—And reptiles.
ROXY	Like you.
FONSO	Lizards?
BERRY	Yes.
EDDIE	Mosquitoes?
BERRY	Not insects.

Eddie pretends to slap a mosquito on Berry.

ROXY	So we have Lizard Brains!
BERRY	Sort of, only sitting under the rest of our brains—the grey matter and stuff—
FONSO	The Ce-RE-bral Cortex! Where you do **math**?

Berry nods.

BERRY	Yeah. And remember stuff.
ROXY	And talk and make decisions.
BERRY	And store memories.
EDDIE	And get ideas.
FONSO	And tell right from wrong?
BERRY	I think so. The very front of your brain, on both sides—

aha! Process, Inc.
(800) 424-9484

EDDIE	What do you mean, **sides**?
ROXY	The brain is sliced down the middle into two halves. You have your left side—
BERRY	Hemisphere.
ALL	What? Globe?
BERRY	Hemisphere. Never mind.
ROXY	… May I go on? … Your left side and your right side—

Using her own head and others' as visual aids. Could draw on a baseball hat.

	—it comes together somehow. Anyways, where all your brain cells are for everything.
BERRY	Except for collecting … and sending messages—
FONSO	Which is done by the Brain Stem part.
EDDIE	Underneath and inside the grey stuff …
BERRY	… Grey matter—and the stem mostly sends and receives …

Getting carried away.

ROXY	—Called the Lizard Brain, which takes over **if** it thinks you're in danger, shouting at once in all directions, "Danger! Danger! Run. No, fight! Run, you fool. No, freeze. Stand right where you are!"
EDDIE	Sounds like my mom.
FONSO	Can it be trained?
EDDIE	My mom?

aha! Process, Inc.
(800) 424-9484

FONSO	The Lizard Brain.
BERRY	I guess, yes. It has to be, yes.
FONSO	How?
ROXY	Why?
BERRY	We would be afraid all the time. Modern man—
ROXY	—And WO-man!
EDDIE	And children!
BERRY	Aren't being chased by giant reptiles or lions or …
EDDIE	… Or horses.

Everyone hits Eddie.

BERRY	Running and fighting aren't our biggest jobs anymore.
FONSO	Says you. If you don't fight for what's yours, someone will take it—and worse, disrespect you. Shame you. Shame your family.
ROXY	Or your friends won't speak to you. They'll pretend you're invisible. Or worse … laugh at you, think you're stupid … call you stupid. Tell everyone stories about how stupid you are.
BERRY	Because you're afraid?
ROXY	Because you don't DO the right thing.
FONSO	Because you DON'T stand up for yourself. Make the other guy back down. Shame someone before they can get to you.

aha! Process, Inc.
(800) 424-9484

BERRY	Trouble is, when you have to run or fight or even think you have to, your Lizard Brain works without any help from the thinking part of your brain.
ROXY	So the fear—check this out!—the thing you fear doesn't even have to be real to send you …
Over-dramatically.	Back in time … back to the most ancient feelings of humankind … back to the Dinosaur Brain. No thinking. No indecision. Raging anger. Immediate response—kill or be killed. Like, it makes **voting** seem stupid to do.
BERRY	Exactly.
FONSO	What if your fear won't kill you—at least not dead?
ROXY	Yeah, just make you **wish** you were dead …
EDDIE	Like afraid of what your dad's going to say, or not say, when he comes home at night.
ROXY	Thought he was your **step**dad …
EDDIE	OK, when Stepdad No. 3 comes home at night. What happens to you then?
BERRY	Stress. When you can't DO anything, run or fight, so you're frozen.
Impatiently. **FONSO**	I'll ask again: Can the Lizard Brain be trained?
ROCKY *Jumping up and down.*	Hey! That's what our report could be.
EDDIE	What do you mean?

aha! Process, Inc.
(800) 424-9484

ROXY	Training the Lizard Brain!
EDDIE	USING THE HUMAN BRAIN STEM BEFORE IT USES YOU!
FONSO	This is excellent. I'll draw some pictures.
ROXY	Donatelli can photograph your drawings …
BERRY	And we can go up in the Computer Lab and put it all on PowerPoint.
ROXY	Wow! What a demonstration. And ... and …
EDDIE	We'll make up the rules.

Everyone stands still.

ROXY	The **rules** for—
EDDIE	Training your brain to handle the Lizard.

FONSO
Turning a box over, pulling a marker out of his pocket ... then a can of spray paint out of his backpack …

I'll print the rules for us.

You guys have to make them up.

ROXY   OK, ah ... ah ... No. 1. The No. 1 rule for training your brain NOT to give in to the Lizard Rule ... IS ...? **IS**?

Everyone looks at everyone else.

BERRY   Maybe we should figure out the rules of the Lizard Brain first …?

EDDIE *Runs around giving* *high-fives.*	Good idea!! YES! Good idea! C'mon, Roxy, I can feel a **C**. YES! Oh yeah.
BERRY *They look at each* *other, then at Berry.*	How about feeling an **A**?
EDDIE	I can do that! Gimme an **A**!
ALL *They do this back* *and forth for a while* *and make it a dance* *before finally stopping.*	**A**!!
EDDIE	Lizard Brain, Rule No. 1: "Kill or be killed."
ROXY	How do we say that so it makes better sense AND keeps Gufferson from thinking we belong to the "Very Bad Gang to End All Gangs"?
FONSO	Forget Gufferson. We could say, Get the other guys before they get you.
EDDIE	Yes. Take care of only yourself, and do it first. Let the other guy worry about himself.
ROXY	"Me first." Survival of the fittest!
EDDIE	Let's save the second part for a workout program. But "Me first"—good! Good!! No. 2?
BERRY	"Never give up anything. Keep everything you have, even if you don't need it."
FONSO	OK … No. 3: "Never be wrong!"

ALL	Yes!
ROXY	"Never, ever risk being wrong. Make everyone pick sides, my side."
FONSO	"Always win! Never admit you're wrong!"
EDDIE	Only "winning" counts.
ROXY	Nothing is worse than losing. I mean, it's better for the safety of your Lizard Brain not to try at all than to risk looking stupid, embarrassed, or afraid.
FONSO	Never let anyone know you're afraid.
EDDIE	Not even yourself. Then you'll always feel safe ...!!
ROXY *Does a cheer.*	... From other Lizard Brains.
FONSO *Pauses. Eddie and Roxy say some of the next lines with him ...* *They all nod, after* **Berry** *does.*	So. I can see that fear is something the Reptilian Brain gives you ... but ... ... if you forget about using the other parts of your brain, then the feelings of the Lizard Brain may not even be true. Is that right?
BERRY	So our first rule for "Training the Human Brain" is:
ROXY	You won't die from embarrassment ... from being wrong or from losing.
EDDIE	But—

aha! Process, Inc.
(800) 424-9484

FONSO	—If you give in and won't try anything because your friends will think you're weird or stupid, **then** you aren't really safer. You are really **only** protecting Lizard Control.
EDDIE	And you may not win, but **if**—
ROXY	You practice—
FONSO	—Overcoming embarrassment AND SHAME …
ROXY	Doing things that give you a brain freeze, until
EDDIE	They aren't so scary, then you can …
ALL	Train your brain!
EDDIE	Train it, teach yourself not to give in to fear, just because you're afraid. Hey, **I** said that!!

*Short victory dance.
Berry slips into his
box.*

ROXY	OK then. I'll make up a Lizard Brain song, maybe a dance. And Berry, you can put Fonso's drawings and lists—and tell the scientific names for things and show the brain model—on that computer program. And put some really cool music to it. And … Berry?
ALL	Berry? Where the heck did he go?!

*Looking around.
Coming to Berry's
box. Peering in.*

FONSO	What's up, man?
EDDIE	Hey, Berry!!
BERRY	I'm not coming out!

aha! Process, Inc.
(800) 424-9484

They all look at each other. They try to get him out. He presses his arms and legs even tighter against the box.

> You got everything figured out. You'll probably even get an **A.**

They roll Berry around with a dolly that Eddie produces from somewhere behind the Dumpster.

ROXY   You're just being a big baby—

EDDIE   Lizard! Baby Lizard!

They try making Berry laugh. Nothing. No response. They all sit down, getting angry. Finally, Fonso puts another box on Berry's head. **Still** *no response.*

EDDIE   C'mon, Berry.

ROXY   Berry, we'll help you.

FONSO   We're nothing without you, Berry.

BERRY   Quit calling me that!

FONSO   It's your name, man!

BERRY   Not exactly!

ROXY   It's also "not exactly" the issue right now.

aha! Process, Inc.
(800) 424-9484

EDDIE	You just got a bad case of "stage fright." Do this; you'll feel better.
FONSO	Yeah, you'll get over it; you'll feel better.
BERRY	OK, if you're so smart, how do you get over your **name**?
ALL	What?! Berry's not such a bad name.
BERRY	It's not my whole name.
FONSO	You're buggin', Berry. Get over yourself.
BERRY	How do you get over a name like Raspberry Beret Johnson?

ALL *Silently. Mouthing what they just heard.*	"R A S P B E R R Y ?"

ROXY	I thought your name was spelled B-A-R-R-Y! Or Beary.

Silence continues. Each tries to keep from laughing.

From the box.

BERRY	Well, it's NOT!
EDDIE	How did you get a name like that?
ROXY	Your mother's a Prince freak, huh?

Evenly, with anger.

BERRY	That's right ...
EDDIE	A what? Prince? Prince William?

aha! Process, Inc.
(800) 424-9484

FONSO	No. You know that skinny little dude with the funky sound? His name used to be The Artist Formerly Known as Prince. Purple Rain? You know ...
ROCKY	Raspberry Beret!! A big hit in the golden-oldie days.
EDDIE	Your mom's a hippie, right?
BERRY	No. But I'm the youngest child, and she says it's my "Karma" to have this name. And I'll just have to grow up before I thank her for it.
ROXY	My parents used to be hippies too. They get all choked up every time they see bell-bottomed Levis and a flower in someone's hair.
FONSO *To Berry.*	Let's refocus here. No one's going to tell anyone your whole name. I never tell anyone my whole name. I don't think I even know my whole name. Only my grandma knows. She knows all of everyone's names and parents and where they were born and who married who. So chill out.
BERRY	Well, I live in constant fear my mother will come to school and be in one of her "I have to really hurry **and** I'm more important than Mary and Moses" moods **and** get me called to the office, with every speaker in the school **blaring**:
ALL **(with BERRY)**	"Would Raspberry Beret Johnson come to the office?! Immediately!"
FONSO	So **this** is why you won't come out of the box?
BERRY *He peeks out.*	No ... Not exactly, I guess.

ROXY   Oh Berry, you'd be worried about not being a **perfect** bag of chips even if your name wasn't a fruit.

FONSO   It's just a Lizard Trick. Like we've been talking about.

Still from the box.

BERRY   What do you mean?

FONSO   You know, it's just the Lizard Brain telling us to run when we really don't have to.

BERRY   You mean I won't be petrified to speak in front of the class?

ROXY   You might still be scared. You just won't have a reason anymore to keep from trying to get **over** being petrified …

FONSO   So then you'll be able to talk or say anything in front of the whole class.

EDDIE   Like now.

All lift the box off.

FONSO

Making rap sounds and a beat. The others follow him, sing-saying:

"Ph'phpp, ba-phpp
bop … jam"
You'll
"ba-phpp"
just
"ba-phpp"
have to find
"ba-phpp"
a way
"ba-phpp"

to live smarter ...
I say smarter
"ba-phpp"
than your
"ba-phpp"
La-Lizard Ba-Ba-Brain,
like a train
in the rain
"ba-phpp"
with the rest of the bus,
"ba-phpp"
full
"ba-phpp"
of the brain st-st-emmed
"ba-phpp"
pa-pa-peop-ple.

High-fives all around.

ROXY
*As they all walk
back toward the
school, carrying
Berry in the box ...*

Face it.

We'll just have to face feeling stupid,
embarrassed, and "petrified" together.

BERRY OK, just this time! But I'm staying in the box.

EDDIE It's up to you, dude. But I think you'll just
feel stupider.

ROXY More stupid.

EDDIE Whatever!

ROXY Are you wearing a box to do the report in?

EDDIE Me?

aha! Process, Inc.
(800) 424-9484

Eddie shakes his head; Roxy points at Berry.

BERRY *He jumps out of the box.*	No, me. This **is** too stupid.
FONSO	So together, especially without the box, we won't be controlled by the dumbest part of our brains.
ROXY	What a great report this is going to be ...
EDDIE	Even for a **C**!

Music from Raspberry Beret comes up as all exit.

Blackout.

aha! Process, Inc.
(800) 424-9484

A Play in One Act

The Lucy Show

Cheryl E. Davis

CHARACTERS

Students in the same Science Class.

BERRY	... not a cool dresser
EDDIE	... surfer dude or dudette
FONSO	... cool, "the bomb" (to kids, not parents or teachers)
ROXY	... whatever ... outrageous
LUCY	... "all that" ... and a cheerleader
TYRA & CHAREE	... Lucy groupies/cheerleaders
MICHAEL	... Lucy boyfriend

NOTE: Remember when you are reading the play you have to decide which gender and sometimes which name to use for each character. There are really only four main characters, but there are eight names, so you can choose which you want to use.

THE SETTING

When the lights come up, we can see a corner of the school library (or media center, as the case may be).

Stuffed awkwardly together are shelves and books and carts full of overhead projectors, suitcases, and machines not always recognizable for what they are used for, plus a TV and a TV camera.

(Most of this may be drawn as a mural: the background as a large cartoon, the library items drawn and then 3-D shaped by being stuffed with paper. They also could be made from papier mache. The TV and TV camera should be real.)

There is a table down and center, with rickety chairs around it. Shelves make a background line, behind the table. Entrance back and forth to the rest of the school is offstage left, behind and around a corner of the shelves. Short stacks of chairs also are visible here and there all over the room or stage.

Berry, Eddie, and Fonso are sitting around one side of the table. Actually, Berry is sitting. The others are half standing around him, looking at what he's doing.

Lights up.

BERRY	If we divide up the work ... the test will be easy.
EDDIE	... This is so-oo borr-ring!
FONSO *To Berry.*	Stifle yourself, Eddie. What do you mean, divide up? Donatelli didn't even give us the answers.
BERRY	You have that wrong. **ALL** we have are the answers.
FONSO	Where's the test then?
BERRY	That's **our** job.
EDDIE	What?
BERRY	Make up the test.

FONSO	That's the teacher's job.
EDDIE	Yeah, that's what teachers get paid for—making up tests so we can't get 'em right, so they don't get blamed when we flunk out of high school.
BERRY	I'm not flunking out—at least not yet—and neither is Fonso or Roxy ... if you'll be quiet long enough to get a plan going.

Whining ...

EDDIE	What about **me**? Fonso and Roxy aren't going to flunk. So I **am** going to flunk, is that it? Huh?

Ignoring Eddie.

FONSO	Where IS Roxy? Donatelli said he would only keep Roxy a minute ...

BERRY	I meant to say "you too," Eddie. Calm down.

Next responding to Fonso.

There were a bunch of girls.
Mr. D kept a lot of kids out of their groups.
Maybe he's going to change her group.

EDDIE	I **knew** something would go wrong.
BERRY	We can get started without her. We'll divide up the chapters ...
EDDIE	And then what?
FONSO	Read 'em. Unless you already have.

To Berry, then Eddie.

I mean, Mr. Donatelli assigned them four weeks ago. And you always **do** your homework, don't you, Eddie, and we all know what a "special reader" you are.

Fonso wrestles with Eddie until Berry stops them.

FONSO   Miss Arlene thinks you're the best **reader** in our class, "Mr. **Hun**dred Books."

EDDIE   Lay off. You're not the world's greatest reader yourself.

Tempers get out of control for just a moment.

FONSO   I don't need to be. I read well enough to get by.

BERRY   Cool it, you guys. You don't have to read science books like a book. There's no beginning or end, just a lot of "middle," and only once in a while does a character show up ... There isn't much plot either; you mostly need to know what you're looking for, then find it. And we have that. Finally, we just have to practice remembering it after we know it.

EDDIE   How can Mr. D give us the answers to a test that he hasn't even given to **us** yet?

BERRY   We split the words up, we look up those words in

FONSO   ... The glossary.

High-fives!

And boom, the bomb, we're done!

BERRY   Mostly. You also have to find each word in the chapter and take some notes on it.

EDDIE   Oh, I bet that's what Dr. Don't—I mean Mr. Donatelli—means by taking notes.

To Berry, then to himself.   Though I never seem to get what he's saying while he's saying it. He's just too weird.

aha! Process, Inc.
(800) 424-9484

EDDIE   I still say **he** should make up the test and give us the right answers. And let us match the answers …

To a key. **That's** what would help us **study.**

Just as they resettle around the table, a rush of people comes around the corner and into the scene. It's more than Roxy. It's more than the three other girlz who enter behind her, though everyone else just keeps going offstage. Lucy and her sidekicks are fashion clones … in cheerleader/preppie hot and expensive.

Roxy, for her part, is wearing all black and boots.

ROXY   Hey—!

Roxy stops as she speaks. The others crash into her and pretend it didn't happen, though they stay behind Roxy, while Berry and Fonso slide under the table.

Whoa!

EDDIE   Donatelli sent the Army—

ROXY   —Nurses.

The girlz act offended.
Make noises of
protest but stay in
line behind Roxy.

To the girlz.
   ROXY   Shu-ut uu-p! ... Thank you.

No one says anything
for what seems like
a long time.

Stepping out.
   LUCY   Which one of you is Berry?

Roxy and Eddie point
at each other, then at
Lucy, who seems to be
expecting something
she doesn't find ...

   LUCY   Mr. Donatello ...?
... and looks around
but not under the
table.

From behind Lucy ...
   TYRA   "E"!
The two look at
each other.

   LUCY   "EE??"

   TYRA   You know, "E!"

   LUCY   Excuse me?

   CHAREE   "E": DonatellEEE! You know.
They all roll their eyes.

LUCY	Whatever. You know, that skinny little man who needs a makeover, has a Hitler complex, and only ever wears denim shirts with a tie, like we care.
*Another **long** pause.*	Well?
EDDIE	Well, what? What about Donatelli?
ROXY *Sitting on the table, pointing at the other girlz.*	They're in **our** group now.
Yet another long pause.	
To Eddie. **LUCY** *Roxy hides the real Berry, who slides under the table too.*	Berry. It's Berry, isn't it? Listen. I'm Lucy, and this is:
Lucy points at each of the girlz, who speak on cue.	
TYRA *She does a little jump.*	Tyra!
LUCY	And—
CHAREE *She does a cheer-clap.*	Char—like charcoal—EEE! Charee!
ROXY *Roxy imitates a little cheer.*	And they have to **"go, win, PASS"** Science this term ... Or they won't be cheerleaders.
EDDIE	Yea! Oops ...

LUCY *Points at Eddie.*	OK, OK, I'm ignoring all of you except … Berry.
TYRA & CHAREE	That's not Berry.

Lucy frowns at them until they change what they're saying.

	That's not who we expected … to be Berry.
To Eddie. **LUCY**	Berry. I'm … we're giving you a chance to be on my … our Science team.
EDDIE *Cheerleaders and Eddie start to leave.*	Cool! Let's go!
ROXY	Oh no-oo you don't. I guess "Berry" forgot the rules.

*Eddie stops.
The girlz bump
into him … all turning
slowly around during
the next speech …*

*Mechanically, like
she is quoting or
reading.*

ROXY	"Every person on the team can add one point to the grade of each team member by maintaining a previous high test score or by raising a test score one whole grade."
TYRA	And all points contribute to the team score, which …
EDDIE	… If above 500 gets the automatic
ROXY	Nutty Buddy ice cream delight …

CHAREE	From Dairy Land ... at the end
TYRA	Of the semester unless ... **unless** ... any member should leave his or her team.
LUCY	Oh, who cares about that? Team points are just ... just immature and **stupid**!
EDDIE	Not if you actually go to school and make it to the end of the semester. They taste better than grades!
ROXY	The ice cream?
EDDIE	Uh-huh. That's for EDDIE—ME. The **grades** are for my mama.

Everyone but Lucy celebrates this. Her reaction quickly brings everyone down. Lucy stomps her foot at her two friends. They immediately separate and stand still ... like they're in a performance line.

LUCY	Well, my grades are for my mother **and** father. So let's settle this. Berry, come with us, ple-e-ease.
EDDIE	I'm not Berry.

Lucy looks as everyone pushes Charee and Tyra back toward Eddie and Lucy ... and the real Berry comes up from under the table and stands behind the two girlz—until they separate and reveal the real Berry.

LUCY
Him?
Berry is red-faced and ready to run.

EVERYONE ELSE
Him!

LUCY
He's too ... too—
She walks around him, like a buyer inspecting a horse. Suddenly, though, he seems to threaten her as they lock eyes.
—short ... He looks like he's still in grade school.

Berry scurries back under the table.

ROXY
Now look what you've done.
Fonso squirms to stay behind him, to stay unseen.

C'mon, Berry.
Lucy, you got a lot of ...

Snaps her fingers at Lucy.
Whatever ... I told Donatelli we'd work with you and your two shadows ... Remember, you know, his speech about getting along as a part of learning in THIS Fourth Period? Well, your attitude and mouth just chain-sawed your big-hair SELF right out of your last chance.

LUCY
It's **your** last chance. You and your "team." Donatelli talked us into being in your loser group. We don't need this. Or you, any of you. My father can hire a tutor **for us—and** he can get me out of Donatelli's class. This fast!

*She snaps her fingers
back and forth and
exits with Tyra. Lucy
has to come back to
get Charee who is
lying across the table,
looking upside down,
staring at Berry.
Berry places his finger
against his lips until
Charee does the same,
only upside down.*

CHAREE   He **is** quite small, you know. Is he really a
... Is yanked off.   Brain?
They exit.

EDDIE   Brains aren't measured by height!

Fonso gives Eddie five.

ROXY   Or hair.
*They all **sit** there.*   OK, that waste is over.
*Sometimes they shift
like they're going to
talk but then look away.
They do this 3-4 times.
Berry, who's still under
the table, especially
is off in space.*   I could go get a box ...

*Laughter breaks the
tension.*

EDDIE   Man, Berry, you know **we** know you're smart.

FONSO   And we know **we** aren't losers.

ROXY   Forget **them.** They're just rich bi—

*Fonso puts his hand
over her mouth.*

FONSO   Rhymes with witches?

Berry slides away.

Roxy's right, though, about rich kids. They
live in another world and think they own
everyone else's.

ROXY   Let them think what they want. We don't need
'em. We have each other. Friendship. You
can't buy that. My mom was a maid in this big
house. Probably next door to Lucy's ... big hair!
Whatever. The rich lady there **thought** my mom
was her best friend. Can you believe that?

BERRY   I feel sorry for Lucy. She doesn't know about
friendship ...

FONSO   ... 'Bout being there for someone ...

EDDIE   Counting on them ...

ROXY   Needing someone. Lucy and her baby-rich
buddies really don't have friendship because
they think they can buy it. I say, Not for sale!

EDDIE   That's the truth. Seriously, man ...

Silence.

*Berry sits immobilized.
The other three get
uncomfortable and try
to get Berry to laugh.
Finally ...*

EDDIE   What's wrong now?

Whispering ...

BERRY	I think I may be rich. Well, OK, my **family** is. Probably. More like definitely.

Dead silence.

Angrily ...

FONSO	Did you make up the part about your name from the Prince song too?

Feelings change to tension for everyone.

BERRY	Why? My family has money. That doesn't make me a liar! Are you a liar?
FONSO	I never let you think something about me that's not ... true ... My family's not rich. I can't believe you'd wait to tell us something important like that.
ROXY	Until we were friends? Check out what you're saying, Fonso.
FONSO	OK. Well, I can't ... I'm not a liar.
ROXY	And Berry's not a snotty snob—or a liar. And we aren't liars either. Chill.
EDDIE	Well, **I** sort of lie, but only if I HAVE to. Never to you guys, though. I don't think. And I don't know if we're rich or poor. My dad says we're NOT. And my mom says we ARE! My stepdad says we are too.
ROXY	None of this matters. The Babes are gone; let's just forget it!
BERRY	So you don't hate me?
ALL	No. No way.

Fonso says this slower than the others.

ROXY	Although you **are** my only RICH friend.
Celebration ...	
	But man, you don't dress like you got any dead presidents in your family.

All but Berry laugh.

BERRY	I don't get it.
EDDIE	You know, the guys on the money ...?
ROXY	Duh ...?

FONSO	OK, OK. Everyone re-chill.
They stop.	Can we study now?
Laughs at himself.	Listen to me. I sound like Berry. Man, if my family found out I was actually studying—my mom's OK—but this is not a very cool thing to do ... for **any**one else I know. You know what I'm saying?
Gestures.	If anyone found out I got **A**'s last semester ... I'd get—man ... Donatelli pulls my report card so it won't get mailed home. I've never even actually seen it myself.
Sincerely worried ...	None of you heard **any** of this ...

ROXY	Hearing aid's off ... What? Hello?

EDDIE	Amnesia! What's my name? Where am I?
Hits himself in the head. They laugh and drag Berry out.	

BERRY	You're not the only one with a secret, Fonso. You own me. The three of you are the only ones besides my family who know my real name—

ALL	Raspberry Beret Johnson!
BERRY	... So—OK, OK ... and no one talks to me like I'm a real person like you guys. We still need to study.

Silence.
No movement
from anyone.

| **EDDIE** | I'm amazed I'm so ... so ready to st-st-study. Yeah, STUDY. |

Moving, finally.
Swallowing.

Everyone moves.
Mood changes.

ROXY	How far did you guys get before the three witches stormed Berry?
FONSO	Not very far!
EDDIE	Except that we have to do the **teacher's** job, that's how far we got!
ROXY	What? What's he talking about?

BERRY

Handing out
papers ...

He can't get over how Mr. Donatelli wants us to study for the test. Here, I've divided up the answers he gave us.

ROXY	Answers? Teacher's job?
FONSO	Get over it! Both of you. 'Splain it to us, Mr. Beret.
BERRY	Hey!

FONSO   Sorry ... you know ... tell 'em the part about how we make up the test questions for the answers Donatelli gave us.

ROXY   Oh, I get it—the **teacher's** job ...

EDDIE   Yeah, and how you don't need to read in Science ...

Everyone gets into position again around the table.

FONSO   Eddie, you are **so** twisted.

BERRY   You don't have to **read** the **WHOLE** Science text like a storybook ... is the deal.

ROXY   Yea, Eddie!

While this has been happening, there also has been a lot of activity just over the bookcase that separates the table from the rest of the library. Lucy, Tyra, and Charee can be seen only by the audience. They have pencils and notebooks in hand and will pantomime active note-taking along with their spying on the table group. They will mirror the actions at the table.

EDDIE   OK, OK, but I still don't get what we're doing.

BERRY	Find **your** words in **this** chapter or in the glossary ...

Turning a textbook over, pointing at Eddie ... The girlz continue to imitate everything the table people are doing.

EDDIE	I gotta read ALL THIS?

Whatever Eddie says, Charee mouths along with him. Lucy nods until she finds out Charee is wrong.

ROXY	What Berry said.

Tyra mouths ... pointing at Eddie too.

FONSO	Were both of you in space when Dr. Don't —sorry, Berry—Mr. Donatelli told us about this?

Lucy tries to mouth along with Fonso, unsuccessfully.

BERRY	Each of us has an equal number of the "words we have to know" list. OK?

ALL	OK!

The three girlz continue to mirror what is going on— except they don't have lists ... Lucy motions to someone offstage,

*then has a conversation
with a tall, athletic,
very cool football/
basketball-type
guy who continues
onstage as Lucy
hides ... Michael
walks in, startling the
table people. As he
enters their area ...*

    MICHAEL   Hey-ey! 'Sup?!
*... Fonso slides
under the table.*

To Roxy ...
    MICHAEL   Berry?
*... who points at
Eddie who points*   Ber-rree! Uh ...
*at Berry who points
at Roxy.*   Berry? Berr-ee! Hey?
*Intimidated by
Michael's cocky
self-assurance, no one
at the table seems
able to talk or move.*

    Ah ... Mr. Donatelli said a "berry" important
    guy would be "berry" glad to help me ...

*Laughing at his
own joke, then ...*

    May I make a copy of these?
... taking the notes   Thank you.
*from each one at
the table ...*   Hang on ...

*... and handing them
offstage. There's a
mechanical noise, a
Xerox flash three times
... and the papers*

come back to him.
He returns them
... and ... exits.   See ya 'round!
Mirror girlz pick up
"lists" as table people
get theirs back ...

EDDIE	It's clear now. Check it out. Fonso? You can come back up.
ROXY	What just happened?
FONSO	Is he gone?
EDDIE	Yeah, yeah.
ROXY	Michael the Ladykiller just cruised our table, and it wasn't even lunch ...
EDDIE	And he was cruisin' for ... ... our **Science words**!!
BERRY	Very, very strange.
ROXY	... And very, very cu-u-ute.
FONSO	Too close ... way too close.

The girlz continue
their silent-movie
version of whatever
The Table does.
This can all be
ad-libbed.

BERRY	Where were we ...?
ROXY	Words ... vocabulary ...

Hands papers back
to everyone.

FONSO	More than vocabulary. Hook us up, Berry.
BERRY	Each of us has to make a test question for every word, every answer—get it?—on the list. SERIOUSLY.

They all just look at each other.

ALL BOYZ (but EDDIE)	OK. I get it.
ROXY	Hey, this'll be easy. What's your first word?
EDDIE	**Mass.**
ROXY	OK, what's your second word?
EDDIE	**Density.**
FONSO	**Volume.**
ROXY	**Cubic meter.** Whatever! Berry? How can I make up a question for a word—or words—that DON'T MEAN NOTHING TO ME???

Imitating Donatelli— in a sing-song voice ...

EDDIE	"Don't say 'nothing' after a negative ... You mean **any**thing ..."

*"Himself" again.
To Roxy.*

WORDS THAT DON'T MEAN ANYTHING TO ME.

BERRY	Ah, ah ...
FONSO	Everything with Dr. Don't is kinda like a game ... a brain game ... trying to check us.
BERRY	... I know ... what he wants ... us to do this for ...

| ROXY | Brain game? *Jeopardy!* ... like— |

| EDDIE | We get the answers; all we have to do is say the **question** ... and WE WIN? |

Like Alex Trebek and a Jeopardy! *contestant.*

"Select a category, please."
"Science, Alex, for '400.'"

Playing along.

| FONSO | ... All square, all over, including all of the inside. |

| ALL (but BERRY) | What is a cubic meter? |

| BERRY | Close, but not exactly ... TRY: What's the space occupied by a cube? |

After looking at a book ...

| FONSO | What is the area ... the space of 1 meter times 1 meter times 1 meter? |

| BERRY | A raspberry! |

High-fives!

| ROXY | OK, OK. I'm getting this, sort of ... except ... whether you make up the question or Dr. Don't does, or if I do, either way I'm a failure. This is useless. I'm still not real sure what a cubic-meter stick is. Even if I can say the right answer. |

| FONSO | Just meter ... no stick. |

| ROXY | OK, I'm not sure what a cubic meter is ... |

| EDDIE | Me neither. But I bet I could guess the right answer if it was true or false, like: True or False? A cubic meter is 1 meter times 1 meter times 1 meter. TRUE!!! Touchdown! |

aha! Process, Inc.
(800) 424-9484

BERRY	We can't write true-or-false questions. They ...

Donatelli imitation.

ALL	... "Don't teach us what the answer **means**!!"
ROXY	Whatever! So ... not a good test ... We need better questions?
EDDIE	TRUE's good enough for me, if it's the correct answer. *Jeopardy!* is boring.
BERRY	Which means we need to know the words, you know, the **answers** better.
EDDIE	Impossible. I'll be reading this chapter the rest of my life.
FONSO	We'll cut the number of words you—
BERRY	—Have to learn about and ask questions about ... that will shorten—

Interrupting Berry, grabbing the book away ...

EDDIE	Cool! Go, Eddie! Go, Eddie! Go, Team! Oh, oh, I know, I know. Oh, oh ... I know HOW. It's NOT that hard ...

Chanting.

"Read ... where you need! Read ... where you need!!"

Feeling Eddie's forehead.

ROXY	Fever: definitely TOO HOT!

Pretending to burn her hand.

BERRY	Read where you NEED ... to ... YES! Go, Eddie ...

FONSO	You don't have to read the whole chapter, the whole—
ROXY	—Huge book ... Just read what you need for what belongs to the answers until you can ask a question that gets THAT correct answer.
FONSO	And then we use our tests—the questions, I mean—to test each other until we ALL can actually remember the answers ... on a test, instead of going blank, finishing the test before everyone else, getting two out of 25 right, and staying in Reading SubA the rest of our lives!

*[Remember, the girlz are mirroring all this, AND they **don't** get it yet.]*

EDDIE	I did this once ... in fifth grade. It's called ... cheating.
They hit him in fun.	Seriously.
ROXY	Teachers give you the questions they want you to know. This can't be right.
FONSO	But without asking the questions, you don't **get a chance** to remember—
ROXY	—The answer, like I was saying ... if you do happen to know it.
BERRY	But ... if **WE** write the tests—
ROXY	—We can teach them to each other ...
She stops and shakes all over real hard.	Oh, ooh, ooh. I'm over that. Weird! I felt just like Dr. Don't. For as long as it takes to multiply 1 times 1 times 1. CUBIC METER.

aha! Process, Inc.
(800) 424-9484

Gets dramatic …

Pauses.	The perfect space you go into mentally when you understand Mr. Donatelli, or …
Pauses.	… the perfect space to mathematically measure this … CUBE … shape. Impossible to achieve perfectly, in reality. Like true love. It's real in your mind where you do the figuring—

BERRY —Formula calculations.

ROXY Whatever. A … cubic … cubic meter lets you … figure out the space … when there's nothing else in that space. Like stuff you can't see—because it's invisible—too big—

Makes a square out of Berry's and Fonso's arms and legs. She points to the space inside their arms/legs.

BERRY Galactic cosmic.

ROXY Or too little—

FONSO Microscopic.

BERRY Or too fast—

Like a movie-commercial voice-over.

FONSO "For the naked eye!"

EDDIE Too fast like … like … oh … man … like … like … the speed of light when you're going warp speed so the Klingons can't blow up your ship.

ROXY Wooo-eee!

Pause.

EDDIE   That is, if we BE the teacher!!! All right!

*High-fives and a
large celebration.*

EVERYONE All RIGHT!!

*And the hidden trio
can't help themselves—
and join the celebration.*

EDDIE   Spies!!!

Everyone scatters.

To Lucy.
ROXY   What are **you** doing here?

To Fonso.
LUCY   Fonso!

He freezes.

**LUCY &
GIRLZ**   Fonso? Alfonso Lopez Malone?

ROXY   Don't change the subject. What the heck are
             you doing here, Lucy? Tyra? CHAR-EE??

EDDIE   Cheaters, man! **Big**-time cheaters.
In a stage whisper.

             Fonso du-ude, go, man. Get out—now.
Fonso stands still. Berry? Ah, uh, uh ... help, man?

To Berry.
LUCY   You? You little—I mean ... You lied to us.

BERRY   Who died and made **you** BOSS?

ROXY   Like, yeah? Who did?

Nose to nose with
Lucy.

EDDIE   Girl fight! Girl fight!!

FONSO   No fight! False alarm! No way!

Calling out to everyone
in the library, then to
Lucy and others.   Beat it, Lucy. Take your shadows with you ...

ROXY   Vampires don't have shadows. Take your show
                and f-fa-fade away!!

Snapping her fingers.

LUCY   Donatelli was right about teams, Berry. Too
                bad you decided on the wrong people for
Exiting.   YOUR team.

To girlz as they exit.
EDDIE   Not fair, man! Totally bogus. Go away and
                stay there. C'mon, Berry Du-ude, we got work
                to do.

Table people get
back to work.

ROXY   Way to go, Fonso! Are you cool or what?!

FONSO   I'm cool. I'm very cool. I just had my man
                Eddie run interference for me ... while Roxy,
                the Cheerleader Slayer, took it to 'em.

High-fives!   Back here after school? Tomorrow?
Bell rings. All nod
and pack up.

ROXY   I hate P.E., especially right after lunch.
                It only makes bad food worse.

EDDIE	Tomorrow, dudes. And I WILL be ready. Roxy, want a note from your mother? To the nurse?

Roxy grabs it.
Starting off.

ROXY	I owe you, Eddie ... Hey, hand-written. Maybe I won't flunk P.E. ... See ya tomorrow.

EDDIE	We BE the teacher: All right!! See ya.

Roxy joins him.

ROXY	"I bee-ee ... the teacher. YES! You BE-EE the teacher."

ALL	"We be the teacher, uh-huh, uh-huh." I said, "Uh-huh."

FONSO	Hey ... see ya ... Make the tests hard.

Berry joins in the rap.
Ad-lib.

Uh-huh ...

ALL	We be, uh-huh, You be, uh-huh, uh-huh, I bee-ee ... uh-huh ...

BERRY	Uh-huh ... Hey ... See ya ... SEE YA!

All exit.

Blackout ...

... for a beat, then
lights back up.

It's the next day.
The Lucy Trio
enters dressed
differently. The trio
crosses the stage

opposite that of
Berry & Co.

LUCY TYRA & CHAREE	It's simple and so easy. Blackmail. Favors. Money talks, girlfriend. Yes, but what is it saying about the test we need to get an **A** on?

Lucy and Tyra make
a face at Charee.
Snap their fingers
and say together …

LUCY & TYRA	Whatever!

*Then **all exit**, as*
Michael enters
downstage. He's also
dressed differently and
crosses back upstage,
going around a table
and is about to leap
over a shelf.

From offstage.

LUCY	Michael?

Michael stops and
turns as Lucy returns
from the direction
she just left.

I **thought** that was you.

MICHAEL	It's ALWAYS ME, baby!

Standing cool.

You need some sugar?

Bends down …
Kisses the air, twice.

LUCY	Ooo-noo, make-up … kisses! Not here, Michael.

Looks around ...

Mummy is a "library volunteer person," which means ... she could be anywhere. And you and I are definitely not a possibility in her book.

With just a touch of bewilderment ...

MICHAEL   Lucy, sometimes you can be so cold ... Is that why you always come over to my house?

LUCY   Not really.

Hits him hard on the arm.

MICHAEL   Owww!!

LUCY   Just don't want you to know my doofus brother ...

To herself but loudly.

To Michael.   Is my Mikey-pooh all upset ...? I'm so-oo sorry.

MICHAEL   Lucy, we live on the same cul-de-sac. We ARE the cul-de-sac. My mother and your mother go to the same hairdresser and club ... We're going to the same private school next year ...

LUCY   I know, but Mummy thinks our fathers

Plays with his face.   should have equal jobs. You know, CEO to CEO—and your father quit his job to buy a ... yogurt stand.

MICHAEL   Dairy Land. It's a franchise ... He owns it. He wants to see me play ball next year.

LUCY   Oh baby, Mummy will get over it ... by next year, I'm sure of that ... Give me that FACE ... you know ... let me see it ... my Mikey-wikey 'uvs 'ucy face ... There ... that's better.

Suddenly businesslike.

I need a favor.

Turns Michael around, pointing   Here.

*toward the library
over his shoulder.*

When he ...   No. Here.

      LUCY   Almost. No.
                        Yes. More.

*... doesn't look in
the right place she
moves his head*   A little more ...
like she was   See that?
*sighting a gun
pointed offstage.*   There.

   MICHAEL   Huh-uh, not really.
Looks around.

      LUCY   There. Yoo-hoo? Trophy case?
Moves his lips.

    MICHAEL   Tro-oh-phy ca-a-se. And I'm ... looking at ...
                     ah ... ah ...

      LUCY   Duh! The "Sterling Scholar 4-Point Forever
                     All Around Best Student Award"?

    MICHAEL   Oh, that ... you're **all that.** Easy. Everyone is
                     voting for you.

      LUCY   Not if I don't get an **A** on Donatello's semester
                     exam. I won't have a 4-point.
*Moving Mike's lips
and face like he was*
saying all this.   And I won't be eligible to run.

   MICHAEL   Ow! I mean, Oh. You mean Mr. DonatellEE's
                    exam?

      LUCY   Whatever.
                     Daddy could only get the principal to make

Donatelli throw my old test score out and give me another one.

MICHAEL   Bummer!

LUCY   Well, I was in shock, you know. I just could not be**lieve** that skinny little Levi-shirt would really give us a test the day after the night of the big game. It's mostly cheerleaders and jocks in Fifth Period. Where **is** his school spirit?

Both freeze on "spirit" momentarily.

So … you know what else he did?

MICHAEL   Who?

LUCY   Don-nie-oh, that Science teacher!

MICHAEL   What?

LUCY   He **ga-a-a-v-ve** the entire class, a-al-l-lll of Fifth Period, geeks and freaks included, another test.

MICHAEL   Your class **all** got a second chance?

LUCY   That's not the point.

MICHAEL   Help me here ... your point ... the problem ...?

LUCY   I'm still not ready for the exam.

MICHAEL   And ... and ...

LUCY   And? And I want you to steal a copy of the test from …

Berry, Eddie, and Roxy enter downstage, their backs to Lucy and Michael. Their clothes are somewhat different. They're tossing a Hacky Sack around. Pointing, but still unseen.

THEM!

MICHAEL Those losers have a copy of the test?! Not for long! Hey! Didn't I already steal this test from them?

LUCY No, you only stole the **answers.** C'mon.

Ducking down and exiting.

Mumbling to himself.

MICHAEL Think your dad could get me moved too? I flunked **that** test. **They** have a copy of it? This is definitely NOT FAIR. I may flunk Science 3 ... unless ... Lucy, baby, this could all work out ... if ... wait ...

From offstage.

Fonso joins the group downstage, and together they cross back to the table.

Blackout.

PAUSE.

When the lights come back up, the stage is empty.

Suddenly from offstage ...

aha! Process, Inc.
(800) 424-9484

LUCY
*Wailing * ... louder
and louder and louder.*

** like Lucille Ball when
everything goes wrong
on the old "I Love
Lucy" TV show.*

*All characters except
Fonso, Michael, and
Lucy—like in a
Keystone Cops silent
movie—cross-bump,
look at each other,
then cross again,
running off toward
the **noise**. Berry is
the first one off the
stage. The rest
follow.*

AAA-a-a-a-a-a-aa-aaoooooow!!

BERRY

Exam grades are posted!

*Stage stays empty for
a moment. Michael
and Lucy enter from
where the noise came
from.*

MICHAEL
*Lucy wavers and
screws up her face ...
opening her mouth
before any sound
reaches the audience,
beginning a very quiet
wail as Michael talks.*

I don't understand, baby. You said you studied
the test I got for you. **I** did.

Oh, don't do that now ... It's just a grade.

You got two correct. That's good, and you still
have a **C** average, don't you?

LUCY   AAAAAAAaaaaaaahhhh!!!
Wailing ... louder.

MICHAEL   Remember, you said the test I took from Eddie
was just exactly what you needed.

*The wailing will ebb
and flow until they
exit.*

MICHAEL   It had all the questions the test did ... that
Berry dude!

In and out of crying ...
LUCY   Not him. Eddie.

MICHAEL   OK, OK, Eddie ... That Eddie guy gave the
test right up. He and the others seemed to be in
a trance or something. I just can't figure out
what happened, Lucy. This was supposed to be
your show. It was all set.

*Lucy hits him and
stalks off, still wailing.
They exit as Fonso
enters down and left,
watching Lucy and
Michael.*

*Roxy comes in from
upstage right,
behind the wailing.*

FONSO   'Sup with them?

ROXY   Seems Lucy thought the test Michael took from
Eddie yesterday was a copy of Donatelli's
semester exam.

Both coming center.

FONSO	**Eddie's** test? He didn't make one up.
ROXY	I know. He was taking the test I put together for us to practice on.
FONSO	I don't get it.
ROXY	Remember when Eddie went off on the other side of Study Hall and was so sure he could get a 100 on the test the first time he took it?
FONSO	Oh, yeah, the one where he got two right out of 25. Yeah?

Roxy starts laughing.

Lucy thought THAT was a copy of THE test? Donatelli's test?

ROXY	Oh no! And she memorized those answers.
FONSO	**Eddie's** answers?

Says very fast ...

ROXY	Eddie's "very wrong I haven't studied yet please let me study now that I know THOSE are not correct" **answers**!!

She gasps for breath ...

FONSO	She won't be a cheerleader now?
ROXY	Oh, she'll be a cheerleader ... She's just out of the running for that sterling doofus award.
FONSO	No way ...

High-fives!

ROXY	Way!

aha! Process, Inc.
(800) 424-9484

Almost off ...

FONSO	How'd Eddie do?
ROXY	He got his **C.** With a plus!
FONSO	You? And Berry?
ROXY	Not as high as you ...
FONSO	Don't tell me! ... out loud.
ROXY	No problem ...

She whispers in his ear.
Then shouting. Ya-hoo! We do the Dew!

They look at each other, then exit.

Blackout.

**The neverending Berrytales ...
Part 3**

A Play in One Act
You Are Here

Cheryl E. Davis

CHARACTERS

Students from the same Science Class. At the mall.

BERRY	... not a cool dresser
EDDIE	... surfer dude
FONSO	... cool, "in/the bomb" (to kids, not parents or teachers)
ROXY	... whatever
LUCY	... "all that" ...
TYRA & CHAREE	... Lucy groupies
MICHAEL	... Lucy boyfriend
OTHERS	... mostly Fonso's cousins, as needed
SHADOWS	... scene changers *

* ... Dressed in one color to blend in with the background, faces painted that same color; they never speak. They are like movable puppet-props, changing the set, identifying what's going on and never letting on that they can be seen.

aha! Process, Inc.
(800) 424-9484

Props/signs necessary before beginning ...
giant, necklace-like signs that read:
THE UNIVERSE   GALAXIES   MILKY WAY GALXAY
OUR SOLAR SYSTEM   PLANET EARTH
EARTH'S BIOSPHERE   ORGANISMS   ORGANS   CELLS
MOLECULES   ATOMS   ELECTRONS   NEUTRONS
PROTONS   PARTICLES

THE SETTING

(For Scene 1)

As the lights come up, we see the back, or the suggestion of the back, of the outside entrance of a typical mall—the loading-dock area, behind the stores next to the movie-complex exits.

Two members of a foursome are just about to go in.

The entrance could be drawn on huge sheets of cloth or paper. (It could be pantomimed—the characters pretending to go through and coming back out.) When the foursome finally goes through the door, the scene changers roll up this "front" and ...

(For Scene 2)

... Turn everything, so the actors appear at first to go upstage, into the mall, away from the audience but end up as the lights blink off, then back on, actually coming through the door, downstage, facing the audience who now become part of the mall and then the theater.

SCENE 1

Lights up!
Two come out talking.

FONSO	Where's Berry?
EDDIE	And Roxy?
FONSO	Lost, probably.

Pacing.

EDDIE	Yeah.
Imitating Fonso	Except Roxy hardly ever gets lost.
in his pacing pattern.	

FONSO	You forget who she's with.
EDDIE	True. Berry can get lost without moving—
FONSO	That's why I said for them to come around to the back.

People come out and
cross the stage, then
go off carrying
packages or pushing
UPS carts, etc.

EDDIE	It's still more people than Berry likes.
	Besides, his mom is dropping him off out front,
	so I hope Roxy finds him before he **freaks**!
	I always thought smart kids had everything.
	You know, had it made ... nothing's ever hard.

FONSO	Like being rich.

Both keep a pacing
pattern going.

EDDIE	Berry isn't exactly predictable, is he? For being so smart. Do you think he's rich? He sure gets lost easy.
FONSO	He also wears glasses ...
EDDIE	Which also get lost a lot. AND he even gets **us** lost!

Slap five back and forth. They both sit on the back of a bench.

FONSO	And gets us **found** too.
EDDIE	But not at the mall!

Running in, crossing almost off.

ROXY	Where **is** he?

Offstage, boys whistle.

They pull her to the bench.

EDDIE & FONSO	Raspberry Beret Johnson?
ROXY	The same. Where the heck is he?
EDDIE & FONSO	Not here!!
ROXY	I left him for exactly two minutes, maybe less. I said, "Stay right here!"

Roxy jumps up ... acts angry.

FONSO	Where did you go?

EDDIE	I smell a boyfriend ...
ROXY *Pushing Eddie down.*	Do not. You just **smell.**
FONSO	But where **did** you go?
ROXY	To the ladies' room; is that all right?!
FONSO	Not for our man Berry.
EDDIE *Pacing ... looking.*	I could be in Arcade Heaven. This was Berry's idea. He has two minutes or ... or ...
ROXY *Paces with Eddie.*	Or ... whatever! Get over yourself. Berry said he needed a big space to show us the outer-space stuff ... that ... Science test ... I hate this class!! I can't even remember what we're supposed to be studying and why anyone with any brains would study science in a movie theater!
Eddie covers Roxy's mouth.	Oh ——!!! We're never, ever ... going to understand anyway.
FONSO	We might. We did before.
EDDIE	Not without Berry. And Donatelli's never going to give us a good grade, even if we **could** get all that SPACE stuff **and pass** the test ...
ROXY	.... **If** we lose Berry.
FONSO *Ominously.*	The mall's closed now, except for the 'Plex. Even the Food Court's shut down. Rox-y-y ...?
ROXY	Don't "Roxy" me. I'm not his baby sitter.

EDDIE I'd baby-sit him. If he **paid** me.

A husky security cop (or two) enters upstage. Members of the group instantly pretend to be reading and talking politely. The cop crosses down, in front of the bench, then goes off downstage. Berry then becomes visible, walking almost directly behind one of the cops. Berry keeps going as his friends do a double take.

ALL Berry!!!

Berry jumps, startled, goes into a ninja position ... then relaxes and runs over. Greetings and hand-slapping, etc.

BERRY I knew it! Man, I thought I was going to walk around this mall forever.

EDDIE Why were you behind the rent-a-cops?

BERRY Well, the sign on the big mall map-thing said,
Catching his breath. **"You Are Here."** But the arrow was broken off.

Then some big guys in black-leather everything and weird hats started toward me ...

FONSO   You do look like a target sometimes.
Eddie does too.

ROXY   Uh-oh, Berry's talking about The Very Deep
Brotherhood of Destiny.

BERRY   A skull and crossbones is not my destiny, and I
was going to talk to them about their choice of
symbols, but then I remembered what Fonso
said about how most people don't really like to
talk ...

*They all gasp and
hold their breath,
letting it out after
Berry finishes.*   So I did ... Fonso's trick.

FONSO   "Walk with the Cop"! Very smooth!!
*They all breathe.
High-fives.*

ROXY   Right alongside, slide! Oh yes!

EDDIE   Du-dude! All ... right!

BERRY   And I figured that eventually the cops would
take me to you.

EDDIE   All right! Take you to us!!? I don't get it.

BERRY   Except they stop every two minutes.
And if they like someone who walks by,
they talk, more than Eddie. And if they pass
coffee or food, they stop some more.

EDDIE   Oh, like Donutsville! Yeah, I get it now!

BERRY   I didn't think I'd ever find you.

FONSO	No, man, we found you. The first rule of being lost is: The people who are NOT lost stay put until they find the person who IS lost.
BERRY	In my family you wait for my mother.
FONSO	The **rule** is: The lost person will walk by, especially if you're on a street corner.
EDDIE	Or at a bus or train station.
ROXY	Or in the mall.
ALL (but BERRY)	Check it out! IN THE MALL! See?

Noticing how cool they are.   The rule works.

ROXY	OK, OK. We're all found. Now what? Huh?
EDDIE	You **got** a **DAH**-ate!

To Roxy, who trips Eddie, then hits him. Eddie winces.   ... dah-ate to get another tattoo, I bet. Now that I am in pain and thinking clearer ...

To Roxy.

BERRY	Hitting people to change their minds is not very civilized.

Going into British accents.

ROXY & EDDIE	Ooooo! Not very civilized, I say!

Roxy hits Eddie.

EDDIE	Hey, wait, I agree with the Berryman!

FONSO
Separating everyone and putting them on the bench.

So, OK. Lost and Found Time is over.

Now what? I mean, Berry, you're the one who said you could use the mall to get us to understand that space stuff Donatelli's been spouting …

Singing the original "Star Trek" theme, in an operatic voice, really wailing.
ROXY

AAHHHAAAAHHHAAHHH!!

BERRY
To Roxy.

Ouch!
What are you doing?

EDDIE

Tripping on the final frontier, man!

ROXY

Sings again …

You know, **classic** Star Trek … "Space, the Final Frontier!"
Ahaaaahahaaaaa!

EDDIE

Roxy and Eddie shoot each other, then rise up and shoot Fonso.

"**We** are the final frontier.
Spock, set your phaser on Stun!"

FONSO
Dying as he speaks.

Kirk.
Spock … The New Generation.

EDDIE

Voyager. Star Wars.

ROXY

Coughing.

They all die dramatically.

Not all those … They just don't have a Spock or a Kirk.

BERRY	Nerd alert!

*They freeze and
glare at him.
Walking and
pointing.*

Sorry. Sorry.
Look, let's just go in over here, in through
the movie exit door—ah ... it's open.

ROXY	It's sure too slow to run another movie tonight.

BERRY	So it'll just be our great big laboratory!!!

Uptight.

FONSO	Uh-uh. They'll throw us out in two seconds.

EDDIE	Or call the cops on us.

Shudders.

BERRY	They won't throw us out!

ROXY	Because you say so? What's up with you, Berry?

Also uptight.

Wanna new thrill, like getting thrown out?

BERRY	We won't get thrown out. Or busted. You guys chicken?

*Makes chicken sounds.
And starts toward the
movie doorway.
They do this **silently.***

*As Berry goes through
the door, the others
follow ... acting like
they're talking, but
there's no sound,
except for the turning
of the vision-line that
marks the doorway,
so that everyone
walks first away from,*

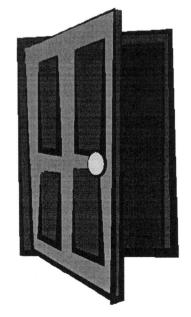

aha! Process, Inc.
(800) 424-9484

and then toward, the audience. Lights blink, as the set shifts quietly, then come back up.

SCENE 2
... seamlessly.

EDDIE *Facing audience*	I've never been all alone in a movie theater before.
ROXY *Starts to hit Eddie Stops in midair, then puts her arm around him. They sit on or at the edge of the screen—or just in front of it. And look around.*	You're not! Unless that Stun was set too high.
FONSO	Well ... unless you got a movie to show ... let's get this on!
EDDIE	Get **what** on?
ROXY	Another science lesson.
Announcer-like voice. **BERRY**	"Space! The Lesson on Space. What is it? How did it get there? The **truth** about gravity!"
ROXY	Wha-aa-at-**ev**er!
FONSO	The truth about passing the test!
EDDIE	That's **my** kind of truth. It just seems stupid to make us come to a theater to get the answers to one of Donatelli's tests.

BERRY	Haven't you figured it out yet? The answers don't mean anything if you don't understand **what** they mean.
EDDIE	I don't **care** what they mean.
ROXY	Me neither. But I know you, Berry. You won't just give us the answers. You're worse than Donatelli.
FONSO	Yeah, Berry'll make us remember what the answers **mean.**

They're all sitting in a row on the front edge of the stage.

This place is bigger without people.

BERRY
He throws a paper at Eddie.

I'll give you the answers ...

Here!

Scrambling ...
EDDIE
Reading intensely.

A'ight! 'S'bout time!
It's an answer key.

ROXY
Pulls out a little flashlight from a chain around her throat. Reads with Eddie.

Berry? Berry, what?

Let me see too.

FONSO
Looking at Berry, who looks away, then at the paper. Confused and excited. To Roxy.

This is new.

What'sup? You steal this?

How many questions?

ROXY

Twenty ... no ... 25.

EDDIE	Multiple choice?
ROXY *Having trouble holding the paper and reading it while Eddie tries to read it too.*	Ah—yeah. Get away from me.
FONSO *To Roxy.*	Read.
EDDIE	The answer is A!
ROXY	Galaxy. Solar system. Molecule. Or atom.
EDDIE	Galaxy!!!!
FONSO	What's the question?
EDDIE *Pulls out a pen and writes on his pant leg. Flips the light to see what he's writing.*	Who cares? No. 1 ... A!
ROXY *Yanking the light back.* *Reading.*	Give me that. A collection of gases, dust, planets, and neb-u-lay ...
BERRY *She looks stunned.*	**La**! Neb-u-**la,** not nebu**lay**.
ROXY	**La** ... that travel through space bound together by gravity.
FONSO	Solar system.

aha! Process, Inc.
(800) 424-9484

EDDIE	Look, man, the answer is A: Galaxy.
ROXY	Planets that travel through space. That's solar system.
FONSO	Yeah. Solar system.
EDDIE	It says galaxy. "A." Galaxy.
FONSO *Reads with the light.* *To Eddie.*	Let me see. It's wrong. A trick. What's a galaxy?
EDDIE	The answer to No. 1.
ROXY *To Eddie.*	What if Donatelli changes the order of the test?
FONSO *To Roxy.*	"Planets traveling through space together": solar system!
ROXY	"Bound by gravity." Solar system!
EDDIE	There's no Planet Nebulae …
BERRY	**La!**
EDDIE	La, la, la! No such planet in our solar system.
ROXY	It doesn't have to be in **our** solar system.
Eddie gets very quiet. To Berry.	Does it?
BERRY	Not necessarily.
FONSO	Point! Next.
EDDIE	The Answer Key says No. 1 is A!

ROXY *Looks at Berry* *who …* *… starts to speak,* *then stops himself.*	OK, No. 2. A collection of particles orbiting in the massive space around a nucl–a, no, ah … nucku-lah. Hmm … Same choices. Solar system. Galaxy. Atom. Molecule.
FONSO	Solar system.
ROXY	Good answer.
EDDIE *Shows them the key* *by pulling Roxy and* *her light to the paper.*	Wrong answer. Look. **D!** Atom!!
FONSO *Reads.*	Give me that. The key says "D": Atom.
ROXY	Well an atom doesn't have "massive" space. A galaxy does.
FONSO	But planets, not particles, **orbit** in space.
EDDIE	Just copy the answers down, and let's go home.
ROXY	The answers may be right but they don't make sense. And I'd rather be wrong than stupid.
Sarcastically. **BERRY**	Good answer, Roxy.
They all start circling *him, the flashlight* *emphasizing this.*	
ALL **(but BERRY)**	OK, Berry. What's going on? 'Splain yourself. Real quick! And 'splain why we're having this study session by flashlight in a movie theater.

BERRY	OK, OK. But you're always bugging me to give you the answers—just GIVE you the correct answers. Donatelli had an old test and key, and he let me take it. And it still didn't help you much. Did it?
EDDIE	It helped me. I have everything I need to ace Dr. Don't's semester exam.
ROXY	Unless he checks your pant legs or changes the order of the questions.
BERRY	Or both. The test ...
FONSO	Exam.
BERRY	The **exam** is about space. Understanding inner **and** outer space.
EDDIE	I know that.
FONSO *Threatening Eddie.*	**Some** of us never came to class much, after the first day.
EDDIE	I know that too. So, moving right along ... outer and—
BERRY	Inner space.
ROXY *Pointing up.*	OK, space, out there. And space in ... in ... where exactly is **inner** space? Is your inner child there? My mom says that's where she is most of the time.

Eddie breaks up.

FONSO	I've been wondering that. And I went to class more than Eddie and Wolfy did.

aha! Process, Inc.
(800) 424-9484

Roxy tries swinging,
but Fonso catches
her head and
as she swings at air.

ROXY	Don't call me that. It's not funny.

EDDIE	To you.

All slap five but Roxy.

FONSO	OK, sorry.

Warning her. Don't even start thinking of names to call **me,** or we'll be here all night.

ROXY	

Clucking. No names ...? OK by me.

BERRY	I hate it when you guys start calling each other stuff.

ALL
(but BERRY)

Shout out different
names (each class or
cast needs to decide
these ahead of time).
This all quickly fades.

FONSO	OK, OK. Inner space. Outer space. Traveling in space. **Lost** in space. Let's hurry up here. What's up with **space**?

BERRY	Good question. And ... the point. That's why Roxy feels stupid.

ROXY	That's why Eddie **is** stupid!

FONSO	CHILL. Right now.

BERRY	She doesn't understand **how to understand** about space.

ROXY
Sitting down.

And ... Eddie **is** spaced!

BERRY

It's hard to understand something you can't see. And except for right around us—and at least as far as our eyes can see—everything's in a space, either too big or too small to actually see ...

FONSO
Enjoys the moment.

Sitting back down.

... With the naked eye. But what do you mean "understand how to understand"? That is **totally** messed up, man!

BERRY
Embarrassed ... Pacing ... The others pace behind him until Berry suddenly turns, and they all bump into each other and scramble around trying to make it someone else's fault.

Oh?
I see that I am not being very clear.

Close your eyes.

All do. Eddie keeps walking and bumps into a plastic garbage can.

EDDIE

Sitting.

He didn't say SIT DOWN and **then** close your eyes.

BERRY
Eddie opens his eyes.

Try to see this theater.
In your imagination ...
Thank you.
Tell me what you see.

FONSO

Darkness.

aha! Process, Inc.
(800) 424-9484

ROXY	Distance.
EDDIE	Nothing.
ROXY *Hits at him.*	Get serious!
BERRY *Silence for a minute.*	"Nothing." Good answer. What do you feel?
ROXY	Air moving sometimes.
FONSO	I can feel how close I am to the others.
BERRY	Can you see the air, if you open your eyes?
ALL *They all open.* *Then close.*	No … Not really.
BERRY	What else can you know without using your eyes.
EDDIE *Pulls out a pack of mints. They all laugh, but in the darkness they can all be heard **crunching** and biting the mints.*	Everyone's **breath.** Certs, anyone?
FONSO	The sound of things. You don't need to see that. But if I didn't know they were mints, I'd think they were chips or broken glass.
BERRY	Sounds, currents, closeness. What about size? Shapes? Descriptions?
ROXY	Everything seems big …?

aha! Process, Inc.
(800) 424-9484

FONSO	Dark.
EDDIE	Empty. A big nothing.
BERRY	Well, people, welcome to **space.**
EDDIE	So what's **inner** space then?
BERRY	... The same. Mostly nothing. Lots and lots of nothing, only so small you can't see that either.
ROXY	Like the cubic meter.
ALL	Oh yeah!
BERRY	Meters, regular or milli-ones (especially cubic meter), is the measure for space and things in it. SI units.
ROXY	"Systeme internationale d'unities."
EDDIE *Laughing at his own joke.*	Cirque du soliel, bien, y tu?
ROXY	The name is French for international units. Measuring in meters, you dummy.
EDDIE	Dum-AY, to you. Besides, I knew that. That's what we had to study for on the last test, which, by the way, I did not write the answers to on my pants ... and still got a **B.**
FONSO	OK, OK. The cubic meter is a big, equal-sided chunk of space.
ROXY *Excited ... upset.*	So, Mr. Italian Unpressed Pants Science Guy Donatelli is telling us that, mostly, space is: nothing.

aha! Process, Inc.
(800) 424-9484

FONSO	How can you study **nothing**?
BERRY	Mostly nothing, nothing's that's very interesting. Except for—all of a sudden out of nowhere—a galaxy shows up full of solar systems and in one particular solar system in the middle of NOTHING is very interesting because that's where we are. And all that is made up of inner space. NOTHING with miniature systems, like molecules and the … the atom and the … the … the particles orbiting in atoms.
EDDIE	And the space in here—in this movie theater? This is mostly nothing too? Nothing interesting?
ROXY	Get serious, Eddie.
FONSO	Look around, du-ude, this ain't **nothing**! This is where we **are.**
BERRY	Now we're getting somewhere.

Pointing …
FONSO	That's right. **You are here.** We are
… all around.	**here** in the middle of everything.

ROXY	Including lots of nothing, here too, huh?
EDDIE	Get serious, Rox.
BERRY	She **is** serious. Space is the place where nothing is … on the way to and around where **some**thing is.

Long pause …

EDDIE	So, what has all this "nothing" got to do with the test? That's what I want to know. A galaxy and a solar system seem to be—way, like—way different from a molecule or an atom. 'Cause those were the only four answers to all 25 questions.
ROXY	Big space and little space.
FONSO	What "space" are **we** in?

Sarcastically ...

ROXY	Re-al-i-TEE!
EDDIE	Galaxy or atom?
BERRY	All of the above. All at the same time. We just can't see it all at the same time.
FONSO	How do we **see** it then—and know it's **there**?
BERRY	First you have to know what place in space you're looking at.

EDDIE *Raps for a minute.*	Ahhh! ORDinary realiTEE ... that's what we see. Can't see inner space ... Can't see much ... Can't see outer space ... ba-da boom ba-da boom ... ba-da punch! With technology, computers, let the cameras ... telescopes see ... ba-da ba-da da ... make the naked eye SEE more realiTEEEE!
ROXY	I just can't see why it takes numbers and formulas to make us see it, whether it's big or little.
FONSO	Magnification, man. One hundred percent bigger and smaller. But at the same time? That's a trip.

aha! Process, Inc.
(800) 424-9484

BERRY	Not if you have a filing system for the size of the space you're looking at. You know, a way to know what goes inside what.
ROXY	You mean … what's always bigger and what's always smaller?
FONSO	Atoms.
ROXY	What?
FONSO	Are always smaller.

All pause ... and look at Berry.

Even when you make them the same size as this theater. In your imagination or under a microscope.

BERRY	Yes.
EDDIE	Oh, like that's going to happen ...
ROXY	Yeah, when the Milky Way shrinks into this same theater.
FONSO	The candy bar?
ROXY	No ... duh!

She smacks Fonso, then realizes what she has done and gets very quiet ... Eddie makes faces at Roxy behind Fonso.

Sorry ... You know, the galaxy. **If** a galaxy could squeeze in here.

BERRY	It can. If we made everything the same size. But we'd need more than a theater, but that's the point. If we could play with the size of atoms and galaxies—you know, like you said,

make atoms and galaxies the same size, so we could look at them better—we'd still find that **in** the universe, whatever point of space you were in, an atom is always smaller.
That's really what the test is about.

Upset.

EDDIE	Exam!
FONSO	Chill, Eddie. Exams, tests, quizzes. It's the same, man!
EDDIE	Exams are worth more than tests. Tests are worth more than quizzes—a lot more.
ROXY	OK, OK. You're right, Eddie. The point is that taking a test or exam or quiz is pretty much the same thing when you're studying.
FONSO	How you study for all of them ... know how they work. It's all the same thing. OK, man?
EDDIE	Well, it's different to me.
ROXY	Yeah, 'cause you don't study for the tests or the quizzes—or come to class. You save it all up and think all you have to do is study for the EX-AMS!
EDDIE	You do too.
BERRY	OK.
FONSO	That's **enough**! Both of you. So: This **exam** is about what's "bigger and what's smaller in the universe"?
BERRY	Uh-huh. And what makes up what ... in the universe of space.

aha! Process, Inc.
(800) 424-9484

Screaming.

ROXY	AAAAAAAA!!! Here we go again. Just when I think I'm understanding all this, then other stuff comes along and makes up even more stuff that is really the smallest stuff **and** the biggest stuff. And the name for all this stuff is—
BERRY	Matter.
EDDIE	And matter is in space. Even if the space is really big or really small. It all fits together and works the same way, big to small, **or** small to big.

Surprised.

BERRY	Ye-e …YES! That's right.

All are shocked.

	The patterns, from big to small, stay the same.
ROXY	He's **right**?
FONSO	He said, "The size of the matter and space is how the universe is put together."
BERRY	So far everyone is right. But it's not going to help you remember the right answers on the test … yet.
FONSO	'Specially if all 25 questions have one of the same four answers.
EDDIE	I know what an atom and molecule … are … mostly.
ROXY	And solar system and galaxy …
FONSO	But we all still got the first two questions wrong.
EDDIE	I didn't.
FONSO	You copied.

aha! Process, Inc.
 (800) 424-9484

BERRY OK. Line up.
They stand still. C'mon, make a line.
They make a line. Let's get the order that these things come in
  fixed in our heads. **Bigger to smaller.**

To Fonso, Roxy,
Eddie. We need more people to make the line.

EDDIE The line of what?

BERRY The universe line.
Calls to the
projection room. Lucy?
No answer.

  Lucy!!

LUCY's
VOICE What?

BERRY Turn the house lights up. And come down
  here. All of you.
Lights come on.
ROXY What's **she** doing here?

Sticking her head ...
LUCY Don't ask, if you don't want to know.
... where she can
be seen.

BERRY I asked her to.

LUCY Did not. **I had** to come or Berry **wouldn't** be
  able to come.

FONSO This is getting very weird.

BERRY Ah-h ...
Eddie runs up and
looks in where Lucy
*is. **They and others***
all scream. I was meaning to tell you this earlier ...

EDDIE	It's the cheerbabes and their boyfriend, Mikey ...
ROXY	Michael's in there too?
EDDIE *They stumble out in their school outfits— jackets, etc.— heading downstage.*	Yup! 'Sup, du-dudes and du-u-dettes?
BERRY *Lucy argues with him.* *Everyone reacts.*	Please come out here and stand in this line. You know, the line I told you about. The one that will help you pass Donatelli's test.
LUCY *Coming out ... with the others and being placed in a line by Berry.*	Exam!
EDDIE *When they line up, Berry hangs labels/ signs on each of them. Berry also hands Roxy a card.*	Yeah, exam!
BERRY	We still need four more people.
FONSO *Fonso will actually pull 4-6 people from the audience or from class as Berry asks him and directs him to. This can be ad-libbed or blocked out. All together there need to be 14, plus Berry.*	Give me a minute ...

BERRY *Pause. Everyone looks at Roxy and then Berry and then Fonso, who nods his head at Roxy.*	Roxy? Do that Star Trek singing thing!
ROXY *Singing …*	What the heck … AAHHHAAAAHHHAAHHH!
BERRY	Now read the card.
LUCY	How come she gets to be the reader? It was my idea to use the theater.
ROXY *Stepping out of line to give it to Lucy.*	**You** can read it. Here. I'll be the background singer.
LUCY *They start to fight. Fonso steps in, pulls them away from each other, and eyeballs Michael, who starts, then stops, coming out of line.*	I don't need any background singing from a Goth-Harley girl.
EDDIE *He glances at the card and quickly gives it back.*	I'll read it. Or … uh-oh … **you** can read it …
LUCY	Everyone line up right. Or it won't make sense.
BERRY *After no one moves, Berry puts everyone in line by his or her number.*	She's right. You're all out of line now.

BERRY	Like this:	
	Michael:	Milky Way Galaxy – 1c
	Cousin A:	Our Solar System – 2
	Charee:	Planet Earth – 3
	Roxy:	Earth's Biosphere – 4 *
	Cousin B:	Organism – 5 *
	Cousin C:	Organ – 6 *

* Every time Berry adds,

"Visible to the naked eye."

Berry:	Cell – 7
Eddie:	Molecule – 8
Fonso:	Atom – 9
Tyra:	Electron – 10
Cousin D:	Neutron – 11
Lucy:	Proton – 12
	Galaxies – 1b
	The Universe – 1a

Checking the order.

LUCY &
BERRY
To Michael.

Biggest system.
"Galaxies" is next to last. Back there.
Universe is last.

LUCY

A-**hem** …
There are billions and billions of galaxies.

*Reading
(giving the card to
others in line as she
gets tired; they give
it to the next person
in line when he or she
gets tired of reading
—and/or the part
belongs to the next
person in line).*

Each galaxy holds billions and billions of solar
systems—planets orbiting around a star, or two,
which in our solar system we call the sun.
Regardless of size, the pattern of matter in

space—from gases and rocks to humans and
their weather on earth … A-hem …
The pattern of matter in space, whatever the
state of that matter: gas or liquid or solid …
The pattern of matter in space, no matter the
size, is a curved system; that's why there are so
many orbits.

Temperature controls the speed of the orbiting.
And if the speed is too fast or too slow, the
orbits can fall apart. But the pieces, the matter,
will get picked up by or thrown into other orbits.

Roxy is singing …
There is singing
throughout.

Next point.

If you go by sheer size and human visibility
and also a pattern from bigger to smaller, then
you can mentally put the different systems—
orbits—in a line.

Getting louder for
emphasis, making
Lucy glare at her,
which stops it for a
moment before Roxy
starts it all over again.

According to the human eye's point of view,
then—from the largest organizational piece
to its smallest (like Russian dolls stacked inside
each other, from tiniest to largest)—the unit
holding all the dolls … is the universe.

Everyone takes a turn
reading all this.

Thanks to telescopes, our eyes can see the next
unit's galaxies. Our galaxy, the Milky Way,
like the other millions and billions of galaxies,
holds solar systems, the next level down to
earth of the universe line.

Solar systems in turn would hold planets to a
particular sun (or two)—all of which brings us
to our own planet in our own solar system, earth.

Earth is the only planet we know of that also contains atmosphere and life, which, if you follow the idea of the dolls being inside each other, by size, makes earth's biosphere the next point in line—the next level of organization. This holds, or is followed (for us on earth) by, the most visible unit of the universe: organisms.

In turn, organisms contain or are made up of organs, which are made up of even smaller units, cells.

And it's at this level that the eye must have another tool, a microscope. Cells, in turn, are made up of the basic elements of the universe, molecules.

Molecules can be plant or animal, biotic (alive, a part of a living organisms) or abiotic (not alive, like water or rocks). And molecules hold the next level of the universe because molecules are made up of atoms.

And each molecule of matter has its own specific pattern of atoms that hold even smaller units, particles: electrons, neutrons, and protons. Particles orbit very much like microscopic solar systems. And each atom of each specific element is orbited by a specific number of these particles.

The Periodic Chart of Elements, hanging in our Science classroom, is a map of how different atoms are arranged by the number of their particles.

And everything in the universe, small or huge, is made up of these same elements or combinations of elements.

EDDIE *Falling down.* *Holding his head.*	**Stop! Just stop!** My brain is drained. I'm too stupid to understand all this.
ROXY *Eddie breathes loudly.*	Just your Lizard Brain. Take a deep breath … This is just a filing system to know where you are and at what level in the universe …
FONSO *Steps out.*	Like in the mall … everything is in here but in different stores, in different areas at different levels, up and down, right, left, and north, east, south, and west. You can only see right where you are, even though the rest of the mall is all around you, all the time. You know?
LUCY	Yes. I get it finally. It makes sense to me.
ROXY	That's because you **live** in the mall.
EDDIE	OK, let me see if **I** get it. I am visible as I stand on earth to me and you … as you.
BERRY	Go SMALLER: We would see inside you …
EDDIE	… As an organism.
TYRA *They high-five her.*	An organism. I knew it! Yea!!!
EDDIE *Walks along the line.*	At the same time? Or is it the same space?
BERRY	That is THE question … I think it's both. I'm sure it's both, somehow at the speed of light.
FONSO	Keep going … as an organism …
EDDIE	… Made up of organs—

aha! Process, Inc.
(800) 424-9484

LUCY	Like skin …
CHAREE	… Made up of cells—
EDDIE	Like blood cells …
ROXY	… Made up of molecules …
MICHAEL	… Made up of atoms—

He and Fonso slap five …

EDDIE	Being orbited … like I said that … all right!
CHEER-LEADERS	O-R-B-I-T-E-D! Yeah!
EDDIE	Orbited by particles,
TYRA	Electrons …
COUSIN D	Neutrons …
LUCY	And protons!
FONSO	The number of each particle being determined by the element you're looking at.
BERRY	While at the same time speeding along
EDDIE	On "Spaceship Earth" …
FONSO	While it orbits the sun.
BERRY	A mediocre star as stars go,
MICHAEL	In our own PERSONAL solar system …

ROXY	Traveling with billions of other solar systems inside our own particular galaxy, the Milky Way galaxy!
BERRY	And from this point where you stand in the biosphere of earth, looking out, you can see other galaxies, with other shapes ...
LUCY	Spread out across the emptiness of the vast universe, as far as the eye can see—
ROXY *Looking curiously at Lucy.*	If you have a telescope.
FONSO	Like the Hubble.
EVERYONE	WOW!!
TYRA	Who knew we could be in so many places at the same time.
EDDIE	And space.
MICHAEL	With so many other things going on ...
ROXY	... Like, all at the same time.
EVERYONE *Sitting and moving about, as cousins return to their original places ...*	Wow! WOW!!!

Pause.

Breaking the silence.

ROXY   Which reminds me of something else that's
going on that I'd like to know more about …

Pause.

How come …
To Berry.   You knew Lucy and her entourage—
Bowing to that
group.   Buffy and Willow and Angel here—would all
be up in the booth?

FONSO   What's up with that, Berry?

EDDIE   Yeah, I thought the first time you met the Lucy
Crew was that time when they spied on us at
the library.

BERRY   Ah—I did—I—mean … yes … that is partly
true.

Moving behind
anyone to get out of
the way … being
followed by Fonso,
then Roxy, and then
Eddie …   I had **never** met Tyra or Charee before that.

ROXY   Who **had** you met? 'Cause you seem mighty
tight … for just meeting these rich, high-flying,
better-than-anybody-else owners of the school.

Berry looks at Lucy.

Jumping up
suddenly.
LUCY   Gotta go! See ya!

Grabbing her friends
and yanking them   Time flies when you're studying … C'mon.
with her as she exits …
They all run
unwillingly   Now!!
off with Lucy.   See ya.

MALL COP

Enters as Lucy exits. What are you kids doing in here? The theater's closed. The mall's closed. This is trespassing— Oh, it's you, kid. Sorry. But don't you think you should be leaving with—

Sees Berry.

BERRY

Trying to get the cop to stop. —Oh no—

MALL COP —Your sister and her friends?

Gasping along with everyone else.

BERRY No-o-o-ooooo.

Shocked.

FONSO Berry? **What** ...

Stunned.

EDDIE ... Does this **mean,** du-ude?

Angry.

ROXY You've been lying to us. That's what it means.

COP This group bothering you, Berry?

Stepping toward the kids as they step toward Berry, blocking them. Back off! All of you. Step back.

BERRY It's OK, Mr. Ryan, they're with me.

The cop steps back and starts to leave.

COP OK, then ... no problemo ...

Eyes Fonso. He exits Just lock up when you're finished.
slowly. Everyone else seems frozen.

EDDIE

After a long, uncomfortable wait begins re-enacting the universe line. Starts out with energy ...

The galaxy, the biggest unit of the universe ...

In particular, our own Milky Way galaxy holds a billion-billion solar systems, right along with our own particular, average solar system that keeps our own particular planet, the earth, in orbit around our own particular star, the sun ...

Tries, but fails, to get Roxy and Fonso to join him in the re-enactment, but Eddie keeps talking, though with less and less feeling ...

Anyway, the planet earth holds the biosphere, which we can see only a little part of at any given time, which holds the organisms— humans, snakes, hummingbirds—which hold the organs inside, which hold the cells, which hold the molecules that hold the atoms of all the elements that make up the universe. These atoms hold the orbits of the particles— electrons, neutrons, and protons—that make up the universe as we know it: biggest to smallest. There you have it; I'm going to ace this test!

ROXY

Eddie, just be quiet. I didn't want to know more about the universe than I know about my **friend,** Berry.

Long pause.

BERRY

All you have to do is remember the universe line tomorrow. And you'll ace the test ... I don't know what to ... do—to say ...

FONSO

Tell the truth. We trusted you.

Sitting down ...

BERRY	You've already figured the truth out.
... and sighing.	It won't matter what I say. It won't change anything.

Long pause.

To Berry.

ROXY	All I've got is **you** figured out.
Angry ...	He was helping out us ... us
Exits.	**poor** students.

FONSO	Shoulda stayed in the box, Berry.
Starts out.	

BERRY	
Yelling at first—	Take the test anyway.
and near tears.	You **can** trust me about science.

Fonso exits.

EDDIE	
Pacing a bit,	
then crosses to	I don't understand all of this.
Berry.	But, come on, I didn't understand how to find my place in the universe 20 minutes ago.

Helping Berry up	
and walking off-	Don't worry.
stage with him.	Fonso will take the exam. We all will. Even Lucy. That'll help us all feel better.

BERRY	I knew this would happen. I knew if you all found out my family's rich and—

EDDIE	And included Lucy the Dragon Woman of the Exclusive Exclusives Club—pardon the rest of us for being alive.

BERRY   Yes, that. Then I knew everyone would stop being friends with me.

EDDIE   Dude, chill. Trusting someone is harder to figure out than getting a good grade on a Science exam.

They exit ...

Blackout.

The neverending Berrytales ...
Part 4

A Play in One Act
Third Period

Cheryl E. Davis

CHARACTERS

Members of the Science study group (what's left of it) find themselves and their enemies stuck in the same Third Period electives class.

BERRY
[BERRY]
... not a cool dresser

EDDIE
[EDY]
... surfer dude or dudette

FONSO
[ALLY]
... cool, "the bomb" (to kids, not parents or teachers)

ROXY
[ROCKY]
... whatever ... Harley look to hip hop

MR. DONATELLI
[MRS. D]
... Science teacher

LUCY,
TYRA, &
CHAREE
... cheerleaders

MATTHEW,
LUKE, &
JOHN
... three jocks

NINE OTHERS
... representatives of other school groups (for example: three nerds, three weirds, three preppies, et al.)

aha! Process, Inc.
(800) 424-9484

NOTE: Remember, when reading the play you have to decide which gender and sometimes which name to use for each character. There are really only four characters, but there are eight names so you can choose which you want to use.

THE SETTING

A stuffy little room used for storage of costumes and other drama and/or custodial stuff.

Curtains are open, but it's totally dark. Bell rings.

Voice over public-address speakers from the darkness.

P.A. SYSTEM Welcome back, students! We hope your vacation break was everything you wanted it to be—
"Sqweeeeee-eeee, pop crackle-eeek!"

There is a shrill, feedback squawk and the sound of the microphone being bumped and touched. More noises. Silence.

—Ah ... what the heck. Miss Beall?

—Ah ... welcome back, students. Advisory teachers will have copies of your schedules. Please be prompt to Advisory. And to all your classes. Standards are high here. Three tardies means Bootcamp D-Hall with Mrs. Ruckelshaus and Coach Leery. There is zero tolerance for tardiness in the home of the Fighting Eagles.

Lights up on an empty classroom. It is littered with desks and chairs. There is a rolling clothes, coats, coat rack, full of clothes, coats, and clothes covered with plastic bags. A door is upper left, next to a chalkboard with rehearsal times written on it. Finally, stools, a sofa, and a podium are bunched together around the room.

All students scheduled for Elective B, in the Cafeteria Annex will go to Room 1C in the Auditorium Wing. All students scheduled for Elective C in the Auditorium Wing will go to the Cafeteria Annex for Third Period. Repeat. For Third Period only. Teachers with Third Period conference time, go to Assistant Principal Stone's office, immediately. For this semester only, Fourth Lunch will precede First Lunch at 10:20. Teachers, please remind students of this change. Ah ... remember, students, you have a fresh slate, except for the students who chose to let their Biology projects go during Second Lunch, right before Break. Be careful what you write on yours! Have ... a great day!

Microphone noise.

**ANOTHER
P.A. VOICE**

Raspberry Beret Johnson:
Come to the Attendance Office!

Laughter is heard over the P.A. until it's switched off. After a short pause, Eddie enters the room, walks around and sits on the sofa. Roxy enters, laughing, imitating the announcement.

ROXY

Raspberry Beret Johnson!

Doesn't see Eddie right away. He stands on the sofa. She's happy to see him. They hug until Eddie falls on the floor.

Hey! Eddie.
Whoa.

EDDIE

Getting up right away
but standing back
on the sofa.   Man! Thanks.
They get awkward.   Hey!

    ROXY   Hey!

    EDDIE   'Sup?

    ROXY   Ah, na'much.
Pause.   You have Elective B?

    EDDIE   Yeah!
Pause.   You?

    ROXY
Sarcastically.   No, I'm hiding in here until Fourth Lunch.

    EDDIE   Cool!

    ROXY
Swatting at him.
He ducks.   Yeah, I have Elective B, whatever that is.

    EDDIE   It's the new losers class.

Cynically.
    ROXY   Great! Just great.

    EDDIE
Happily.   That's j'st what I was thinking. Cool!
          A totally losers class!

    ROXY
Walking around.   NOT!

    EDDIE   No homework.
Watching Roxy, but
he stays standing on
the sofa. Bell rings.   Are you talking to me now?

aha! Process, Inc.
(800) 424-9484

ROXY	No. You're talking to me.
EDDIE	I can be down with that.

Sits.

Fonso enters. Doesn't see Eddie at first.

FONSO	Hey, Roxy? 'Sup?
ROXY	Fonso. Look'n good!
EDDIE	

Almost popping up between them.

Fonso!

To Roxy.

FONSO	We talk'n to him yet?
ROXY	'Bout what?
EDDIE	She is. Well not totally, but I'm down with that.
FONSO	

Laughing a little.

Cool … **cool** with that.

EDDIE	Good. Ah, cool. I'm cool with that. You know me. I'm always cool.

Nervously. Too fast.

Please talk to me. It's not my fault Berry's related to Lucy.

ROXY	You knew.
FONSO	You **knew,** man!
EDDIE	Not until **you** did.
ROXY	Whatever!

Moves away from both.

FONSO	Elective B, huh? Wonder what it is?

aha! Process, Inc.
(800) 424-9484

EDDIE	It's a losers class.
FONSO *Getting angry.*	I don't take no "losers" class, man.
EDDIE	Oh no, man, not you … I mean …
ROXY	He means us.
EDDIE	I just mean me, I guess … All I mean is, you know … They gotta fill a time slot. So, abracadabra, we get: ELECTIVE B!

Three jocks enter.
Stand, look around.
One goes out and
checks the room
number and returns.

JOCK A *To Jock C.*	This is it.
JOCK B *To Jock C.*	What a hole.
JOCK C	Elective B, man. It's always like this.

Long silence.
Everyone takes turns
looking at each other
when no one else
is looking.

EDDIE *Moving off sofa as* *jocks sit.* *To Jock C.*	You had this before too?
JOCK C *To Jock B.*	Tell Skater Boy to sit down.

JOCK B
Jock C helps lift Eddie up in the air, preparing to drop him. Fonso stands. They carefully set Eddie on the floor.

Please sit **here,** Skater Boy.

JOCK A

Fonso, man. 'Zit goin'?

FONSO
Sitting next to Eddie.

'Sgoin'. You?

JOCK A

Cool.

Looks at others, gets less friendly.

We're ... cool.

JOCK C
To Roxy.

Hey, baby ...

ROXY
Stands, turns, and re-sits upstage, while staring at Jock B.

That was **so** intelligent.

EDDIE

Good one, Roxy.

JOCK
Standing up, then sitting and laughing.

Yeah ...

Good one, Ro**X-x-**y.

DONATELLI
Entering, slamming door and dropping papers on jocks. Papers blow all over.

Oh, sorry.

*Everyone chases
after them, putting
the papers in a pile
on the student desk
that Donatelli is
stacking things on.
Acknowledges jocks
by name, instead of
A, B, C.*

Thank you.

OOPS! Sorry. Thank you. And you.

Matthew, sorry. Thanks, Lucas. I'll take that, John. Thanks, Eddie. Thank you, Roxy, Fonso. There. I guess there's no way to make another entrance. Lucas?

JOCK A   Luke.

DONATELLI   Sorry. Ah, Luke, go down to Assistant Principal Stone's office and ask his secretary for the class roll for Elective B.

LUKE   Sure.

*Exits …
… as everyone else
takes turns reacting
to Donatelli and
"Elective B."*

EVERYONE   Oh no! Not Science!!

DONATELLI   Oh. No? No. NOT Science.

*They all re-sit as
several more students
from different groups
enter, crowd in, look
around and sit down,
all trying to sit or
stand in the same
space by the door
until Donatelli can't
quite be seen.*   I said, "Not Science." Drama.
*There is one huge
clump of students.*

aha! Process, Inc.
(800) 424-9484

The rest of the cast comes in during this confusion and stays behind everyone else. This is almost a pantomime parade of how different groups identify themselves in school.

[Each cast will have to carefully decide and dress this scene to make the point.]

Luke comes in, elbows his way through the multitude, and gives the class list to Donatelli.

LUKE   Mr. Stone said to check if everyone was officially signed up. If they aren't on this list, they have to go to Stoner's office RIGHT NOW and get registered.

To Donatelli.   Is this really a Science class?

ROXY   Is this really a Drama class?

DONATELLI No.

Most students react negatively.   Yes.
A few students react positively ...
Everyone is standing and milling and talking.   FREEZE!
Everyone but Eddie stands perfectly still.

Donatelli grabs him by the collar until he is standing still.	GOOD! No one move! I see you all know what that direction means. Keep free-e-ezing!
Looks at class list.	Count off, starting with Fonso.

FONSO
He touches Eddie.

One!

EDDIE

Oh—TWO!

FONSO
To Eddie.

Touch and I'll count.

DONATELLI
Preoccupied, looks up.

Excellent teamwork. The rest of you stay "FROZEN" until there's a complete count.

FONSO

Three!

Eddie lifts each student's hand as Fonso counts.

Four. Five. Six.

Turns to face audience as he finishes the count. We only hear the last numbers.

Seventeen. Eighteen. Nineteen!

EDDIE

Check.

DONATELLI

Looks at list, then class. Class stays "somewhat" frozen.

Nineteen. OK.

Malone. Torres. Pinnelli. B. Johnson. Stay! Everyone whose last name I did NOT call … leave your stuff and go to Assistant Principal Stone's office.

There is some hesitancy.

Now. Go. Go. Go. You are **not** registered!

Group thins out and exits slowly. Mumbling.

DO NOT COME BACK HERE without your registration slip.

To Lucy.

Yes, you … go.

Roxy turns around quickly and comes back. Members of the Science foursome are the only students left.

Not you, Roxy.

Well. This feels like Fourth Period.

ROXY   Not for long. I'd rather take P.E. than Science.

DONATELLI Drama.

ROXY   Whatever.

DONATELLI Unless you want to take three buses across town. This is your last choice. There isn't even a Study Hall open. Why do you think I'm teaching "Intro to Theatre Arts"?

There's dead silence.

Berry is way upstage by the door. He won't look at anyone, not even Donatelli. Roxy faces away from Berry, and only Eddie is looking around.

This is the only Third Period class left, at least until mid-term.

ROXY   That's NOT very fair.

DONATELLI Oh, I don't know. Seems to me this is the perfect Third Period for you. All of you.

FONSO   I don't want to take a theatre class, even from you, Mr. D. And I sure don't want to be in a class with Berry Two-Faces or his sister!

DONATELLI I'm going to need your help, if you don't mind. And, like I said, there aren't any other choices. Well … I was wrong.

Looks at paper again. There **are** three openings in Sewing I.
Silence. Berry, do you have anything you'd like to say
to Fonso and Roxy here?

*Everyone mills
around feeling
uncomfortable,
pushing Eddie off
the sofa. They
sit down.*

BERRY
Standing, then being I'll take the Sewing class.
*pushed back down
by Eddie.*

EDDIE I can't believe you, man. You may be good
with machines, but you've never taken on Miss
Warnikowski's 1972 sewing machines.
B'sides … You **do** owe all of us an explanation.

FONSO So 'splain it to us, Berry.

ROXY I'm outta here.

DONATELLI Oh, sit down, Roxy. You came to me just
yesterday to get me to arrange a meeting with
all of you.

ROXY Mr. Donatelli!!
Acts embarrassed.

**EDDIE &
FONSO** Roxy?

BERRY Is that true?

DONATELLI Ask Roxy. I've got to go make sure everyone
in here gets to Stone's office and back. I don't
care if you talk to each other. Just don't leave
the room until I get back.

As he exits ...

And I **will** write you up, if you leave. And I **will** come and get you, wherever you hide, and make you stay for detention WITH ME ... if I DO have to write you up.

Leaves.
Comes right back in
to get some papers.
Finally off.

Then you'll have to explain these temper tantrums and pouting to **me,** until I **get** it.

Silence.

More silence.

Breaking the silence
together at the same
time, almost.

      BERRY   It's all a big mistake.

      ROXY   Start talking, Berry.

      EDDIE   Go, Berry. Go, Berry!

      FONSO   Whose mistake?

Silence again.

More silence.

All start talking
together until no one
can hear. Then they
take turns.

      ROXY   I can't hear you. Whose mistake?

      EDDIE   Go, Berry! C'MON, MAN.

      FONSO   Start talking or take Sewing, I don't care.

      BERRY   My mistake. I'll just take Sewing.
Starts to exit. Fonso
and Eddie stop him.

FONSO   Oh, no you don't. If we don't work this out, Donatelli will talk to us.

EDDIE   Separately …

ROXY   … And together.

FONSO   He might even bring our families in on this … My grandmother won't come, but she'll never leave me alone if Donatelli calls her.

ROXY   My mother would just love to call my father up and make him fly down here because I am so **"unruly"** again.

EDDIE   My father—OK, Stepdad 3—would wake up long enough to make my mother come to school and then **I'd** never get over that.

BERRY   And **my** mother is already at school (she's probably still in the building) ready to take care of her "little Raspberry."

OTHERS   Oh yeah!
Imitating P.A.   "Would Raspberry Beret Johnson come to the Attendance Office?"

They all laugh together.

Then silence again.

BERRY   Look. The only thing that has changed is that you know Lucy is my sister and my parents have money.

EDDIE   My parents have money.

FONSO   Mine too.

ROXY   Oh, yeah, we **all** do. But yours, Berry, are filthy rich.

FONSO	And you should have told us who you were—from the very beginning.
BERRY	Because I'm a rich snob, just like my sister?
EDDIE	Not exactly.
ROXY	Yes, exactly!
BERRY	What does it change?
FONSO	A lot.
ROXY	It changes everything, really.
BERRY	About me? About who I really am?
THE OTHERS	No!
ROXY	Yes. No.
BERRY	No!
FONSO	By not saying anything, you **lied,** man. I trusted you.

BERRY
Thinking about what Fonso just said, then crying almost.

Silence.

I'm sorry. I am **so** sorry! …
But I said that. So tell me … what has changed?

What is different? About me? And you and me … all of us … being friends? What do I need to explain?

EDDIE	For one thing, and I'm just speaking for myself, but … if you're so rich, and Lucy is really your sister …

ROXY	And you really live on Mansion Crest Row ...
EDDIE *Points at Berry, waving at his clothes.*	Then ... how come you dress ... Like that?
FONSO	Like you were poor.
ROXY	Yeah.
BERRY	That's exactly what my sister and mother and father and grandparents ask me. Why? Why do I dress like I'm from "the other side of town"?
EDDIE	Which side? The apartments? Uptown?
ROXY	... The Projects? Riverside?
FONSO	The trailer park? Behind the bank? Chinatown?
EDDIE	Fourth Street?
ROXY	Little Saigon? Martin's Creek?
FONSO	Burkefield? That other condo complex?
BERRY	Nowhere. I don't dress from anywhere. I just like to wear certain things. Whatever. My clothes just feel good to me. I don't care where **you** dress from. Or how you dress. Any of you.
ROXY	Because we all look good. Anyway, your sister is Miss Preppie of all time.
BERRY	So?
ROXY	I just thought. Well ... rich people are all the same, man. You can't trust 'em. They always look down on you. Lucy sure does.

aha! Process, Inc.
(800) 424-9484

EDDIE	She even looks down on other **rich** people.
BERRY	You know, **I** had doubts about being friends with you … all of you. Mr. Donatelli said, "Don't worry. Once they get to know you, they'll see past anything on the outside. Trust me! I know these kids. They hate people judging them. They won't judge you. Even if they find out about Lucy."
ROXY	He told me practically the same thing.
FONSO *They sit closer to Berry.*	Me too.
EDDIE	Not me. He never tells me anything—oh, ooo, oh. Yes he did. He said if I didn't come to school every day, I would mess up everyone else's grade. So I did.
ROXY	What?
EDDIE	Come to school.
FONSO	I thought I saw you more often. Whose grade?
BERRY	Our Science grade last term. The big test and project. You know …
FONSO	You came to school … for us?
EDDIE	Totally cool, huh? And Dr. Don't threatened to call my dad—at home—in the daytime. My mother doesn't know he's there these days. And my mom, if she found out he was home, she'd blame it on my skateboarding. It's like **anything** is a good enough reason to blame it on my boar-r-rd, man. I sure didn't want to have to get another board.
They all nod.	
	And I got a **B** on the test!

aha! Process, Inc.
(800) 424-9484

They high-five him.

ROXY	I just don't like rich people. They don't understand regular people.
FONSO	You mean **poor** people. The rich don't think they're better than **every**one else—just poor folks.
BERRY	Some do. Most just don't think. They figure everyone thinks the way they do. Poverty is, like, totally invisible to most of them. They just think that what they have and feel is the same as everyone else. Maybe all of us do that.
ROXY	OK, maybe I wouldn't like Lucy, even if she dressed—
EDDIE	Totally Harley.
ROXY	Or Goth or anything. And Berry, you aren't like her.
FONSO	You aren't like **any**one, really.
EDDIE	None of us are. My skateboard friends think I'm crazy to come to school every day.
FONSO	None of my friends know I've been getting all **A**'s.
EDDIE & **BERRY**	Way to go!
FONSO	I can't tell my family—or my other friends—that I'm friends with you guys either. They'd say I forgot my blood, my pride. They'd only see you, all of you, for what was on the outside. Just like I did with Berry. And by how I see Lucy and her friends. I didn't think I was prejudiced. I just thought everyone else was.

Silence.

ROXY

Silence.

You've been getting A's?
Me too. And if you tell anyone, I'll have to have you rubbed out. Berry, I thought you should apologize to me.

ROXY

And I thought I would never accept your apology, if you did. Color. Money. Having a father. I guess everyone gets blinded by what's different and doesn't know it.

To Roxy.
EDDIE

Are **you** giving **Berry** an apology?

ROXY

Hits at all the others. Whatever!

Donatelli bursts into the room, talking to someone behind him.
DONATELLI

Nineteen is the total number. This room holds 10.

Closing the door.

OK. Looks like we'll be the only ones in class today. The computer doesn't seem to recognize anyone but Dr. Vesco.

Looks around.

Anyone still need to talk?

ALL

No. No. We're all talked out.

DONATELLI

Good.

Pacing.
ROXY

What is this class anyway?

DONATELLI

Drama ... Theatre Arts.

Quizzically.
BERRY

I thought you were a **Science** teacher ...

Casually.
DONATELLI

I am.

FONSO	Did you get fired?
DONATELLI	No, definitely not fired. More like "hired."

*Students move toward
him as he finishes.*

	This is my conference time.
The substitute for Mrs. Snyder—
BERRY	You mean Miss Esterman?
DONATELLI	Nope. She got married and became Mrs. Snyder last year. Had her baby last term.
ROXY	Oh, Mr. Marks, the guy who took Snyder's place …
DONATELLI	Him. He moved to the Middle East—to teach at an oil refinery or something. Anyway, there aren't any long-term subs. So I got the short stick.

*They all look
confused.*

	It's just a way of saying … I got the job.
ROXY	As the Drama teacher?
EDDIE	Bummer.
DONATELLI	Nice word choice. But I have an idea. At least I did when I saw the four of you were taking this elective in Third Period. But first, are all of you—

Looking around.

	—OK with each other?
ROXY	We're over ourselves, if that's what you mean …

They all agree with her.

DONATELLI	Great! I want you to be my co-teachers.

*Silence, then …
Mumbles.*

ROXY	Huh?

EDDIE   What does **"co"** mean?

FONSO   We teach this class **for** him. I think …

DONATELLI With. **With** me.

ROXY   Really?
Starts to get excited,
then "catches" herself. Whatever. It beats Sewing.

BERRY   Got that right. But is it legal?
Long silence.

DONATELLI Well, they said I could get whatever help I
wanted—as long as it didn't cost anything. Every
one of you has had a Drama class. Some of
you had this same Drama elective—excuse me,
Introductory Theatre Arts class—more than once.

FONSO   The teacher never liked me.

ROXY   Me neither.

EDDIE   She **loved** me. I don't know why I kept flunking.

BERRY   I got sick.

FONSO   Last term? You weren't sick for Science.

BERRY   I get migraines. They come on all of a sudden.

ROXY   Don't make me get a box for you to hide in,
Berry.

DONATELLI OK. You all missed too many classes, or were
terminally tardy, to pass this class. OK?

EDDIE   All right, du-udes!
High-fives everyone.

DONATELLI	Take a bow too, Roxy. You and Eddie both took "tardy" to a new level.
ROXY *She bows. The others applaud.*	The class was stupid. It still is. I've already done this class at my old school, only they wouldn't give me credit for it here. Because it was called something else.
BERRY	I still want to know … If we help, is it, you know, legal?
ROXY	Relax, Berry.
DONATELLI	Say what you mean, Berry.
BERRY	What do you know about Drama? Or Theatre?
DONATELLI *Berry nods. The rest pay attention.*	Do you mean, Can you trust me if I want **your** help? OK. Let's see … I've been in a lot of plays. Painted a lot of sets. Written a couple of shows. Directed a little. And I'm an expert on two things: teamwork and "Figuring Out How Students Learn Better."
FONSO	And Science.
EDDIE	And turning students into the teachers.
DONATELLI *Singing.*	My point exactly. "Doncha want to be the smartest you can be?"
ROXY *Singing.*	Please don't start that Army song …
ALL (but ROXY) **ROXY** *They stand at attention.*	"Be all that you can be!!" Stop. Please. Ten hut!

To Donatelli.	Sir, my father was a colonel before he retired. Sir! Reporting for duty, sir!
DONATELLI	OK. Here's my plan. How long before the bell rings?
EDDIE	He's talking to you, Berry.
BERRY	About 20 minutes.
ROXY	How do you **do** that?
FONSO *Pulling Berry's sleeves up.*	Magic. Nothing up his sleeves.
EDDIE	Born with time in his head.
ROXY	Cut it out! OK. Twenty minutes.
DONATELLI	I want you to help me write the curriculum for this class.
EDDIE	The **what**?
BERRY	How?
EDDIE	No way. **Curriculan.** Too hard.
To Eddie. **ROXY**	Curricu-**lum**!
EDDIE	It's a teacher thing.
FONSO	Sounds hard and not very fun.
DONATELLI	It's a fancy word for what we need to know and how we're going to know it—
ROXY	I got it! I got it: DRAMA FOR DUMMIES!
FONSO	That's a better name than Elective B for Track 2 students.

aha! Process, Inc.
(800) 424-9484

EDDIE & **BERRY**	No kidding.
ROXY	Tell us what to do.
DONATELLI	I need some long sheets of butcher-block paper. Felt-tip pens. Tape.

They stare at
Donatelli. Then
at each other.
And point to the
chalkboard.

What was I thinking? Chalk is good.
Chalkboard ...

Touches it.

Old, ancient chalkboard.
OK. There are 19 students—22 by the time
registration settles down. We have no stage.
A lot of costumes ...

Dust flies off when
he touches them.

Or not ... hardly any room in here ... no desks ...

EDDIE	We got a **sofa** ...
DONATELLI	Good enough. Now, what does everyone need to know to get an **A** in Introductory Theatre Arts?
FONSO	And what do they need to know about their teacher?

High-fives!

DONATELLI	Rules. Yes. Let's brainstorm some more topics.
ROXY	Acting.
FONSO	Stage positions.
EDDIE **BERRY**	Lines. Embarrassment.
ALL	Yes!
DONATELLI	Handling embarrassment. Perfect.

aha! Process, Inc.
(800) 424-9484

BERRY	This sounds just like Science.
EDDIE	We gotta teach 'em about the Lizard Brain.
ROXY	In Drama?
FONSO	It's brainstorming, Roxy. No wrong ideas yet.
ROXY	Whatever!
BERRY	Readers' Theatre.
ROXY	Plays.
EDDIE	Comedy. YES! "Whose Line Is It Anyway?"
DONATELLI	Improvisation. Improv.
FONSO	Choral reading. Plays.
ROXY	News.
BERRY	Broadcasting.
FONSO	That's not acting.
ROXY	Remember the rules, Fonso. It's not the right time for criticizing. We're brainstorming!
BERRY	Duet acting.
ROXY	Yes, we could even do competitions.
FONSO	That's what we'll do for grading.
DONATELLI	Competitions?
FONSO	Yes, like first and second and third places. Medals.
BERRY	Certificates.

ROXY	Oscars!
EDDIE	Points.
ROXY	For what?
EDDIE	I don't know. Teachers always say that.
DONATELLI	We do?

They all agree.

FONSO	I got about 100 million points in school so far.
BERRY	I used points in Burton's class to go on a trip.

He is standing on a box so he can write all the ideas on the board.

EDDIE	Gifted kids always get to go on trips.
BERRY	If they earn enough points.
ROXY	In private school the points are money.
FONSO	You are so full of yourself.
ROXY	What—
OTHERS	—ev-v-ver!!

They all go a little nuts.

DONATELLI	OK, you got the idea. Are you with me?
OTHERS	Yes! Hey, hey, we say. All the way with Don-a-tell-AY!!

Dancing and making a lot of noise.

DONATELLI	Meet me in here—after school.

ROXY	Can we set up the room how we want?
DONATELLI	Will it help everyone in class get an **A**?
FONSO	Not everyone will earn an **A**.
EDDIE	Heck, we'll just give everyone who comes every day an **A**.
BERRY	No can do. The state has rules, you guys. No free grades.
DONATELLI	The teacher's job is to make it possible for all students to get an **A** … to know the stuff and how to study for it. And pass it.
EDDIE	I'm taking you with me to my Math class. That du-ude said only 10% of us could get **A**'s. And 10% were supposed to flunk, but our class was below the state norm: More of us would flunk and get **C**'s. Mrs.—
DONATELLI	DON'T TELL ME!
ALL	We know, "Don't tell you. Go tell **that** teacher."
EDDIE	Sorry.
DONATELLI	Do you get my point?
ROXY	It will help us all get **A**'s. It'll make it easier to learn about theatre. I promise. I'm even going to get Lucy to help me. She's in here too. I saw her and the Shadows.
BERRY	That's not my fault. My mother convinced the principal that the last teacher was a total incompetent—and that her children and their IQs shouldn't have their precious records scarred with **F**'s.
DONATELLI	That's way more than I wanted to know.

aha! Process, Inc.
(800) 424-9484

ROXY	See what I mean by rich people?
EDDIE	My dad called Mrs. Favor. I think.
ROXY	OK, so did my mom. At least she said she was going to. Maybe it's not just a rich thing.
FONSO	Mine didn't.
DONATELLI	Three out of four—

ROXY

She and Fonso glare at each other for a moment.

What if you told anyone at your house you were in Drama class …?
No wonder no one called the school.

DONATELLI	Meet me back here. Right after the last bell. OK?
ALL	OK. OK.

Blackout.

Then lights right back up. Roxy, Lucy, Tyra, and Charee are cleaning up the room. The costumes are gone, posters are up. There is a portable roll of butcher-block paper, pink in one corner, and a bucketful of markers, tape, etc.

ROXY

She has a T-shirt and shorts on over her black outfit, and she is barefooted. She drags it back and forth across the tiny space of the room.

Pull the couch—

—o-v-er-er-r-r here.

Lucy and the others stop to watch. They stand opposite of Roxy and her actions.	No. Her-r-re.
And they walk and stand like they're modeling. *To the others.*	No. There. There. No. You could help.
LUCY	Only if you let us drag it to the garbage.
ROXY *She lifts a cushion and pushes it at Lucy. The others smell it until Lucy pushes them away.*	It's not dirty. Smell! See?!
TYRA	Smells clean.
CHAREE	Uh-huh!
LUCY *They all nod and agree, even Roxy for a second.*	Duh, it's u-ug-ugly!
ROXY *They all slap five. Lucy hesitates but does.*	It would set ugly back 10 years!
LUCY *Pulls out a cell phone. The others sit on the couch and watch. Shakes her head and makes an "L" with her free hand on her forehead.*	It just won't do. "Kasha! Yes. Yes. Uh-huh. Yes, it's Miss Lucy. Like, Das Vadonya, uh-huh. OK. Kasha … Kasha. Pu-l-l-le-ease! Get Maria. MA-REE-A!

	Yes, Maria. Now. Oh Maria, thank God, I didn't think she'd ever get you. I know … I know … he never shuts up. I don't know how you put up with it all day. I'm glad to go to school … Yes, I am wearing that mauve outfit … Thank you. Listen. I need you to get Phillip to go to … I need a **black** sofa throw. A big one … Have him go to … to … Wal-Mart?
Looks at the others.	'EEEE, LOOK!' And bring it to room— —the front of school. I'll have someone come and get it. OK.
They shrug.	Love you too. Bye!" OK, the couch problem is solved.
ROXY	Who's Kasha?
LUCY *While sending Tyra out to pick up the throw.*	This maid we just got. She doesn't speak English. None. And! She thinks I look like her daughter Papeshka or something. At least that's what Maria told me.
ROXY *Lucy laughs for a long time.*	You call your mother Maria?
CHAREE *Charee and Lucy laugh.*	Maria is the nanny. Duh?
ROXY *Starts dragging the couch and other stuff around.*	Whatever!
LUCY	Who do you think Phillip is?
CHAREE *Laughs some more.*	Her dad?

aha! Process, Inc.
(800) 424-9484

Sincerely.

LUCY	You have a great sense of humor, Roxy.
ROXY	So do you, Lucy. So do you. Is she Berry's nanny too?
LUCY	Not exactly. Berry is sort of "Mother's Pet Project." Grandma thinks Mother had empty-nest syndrome early, and Berry is just her way of handling my growing up. Actually Berry spends all his time in his room on that computer doing who knows what. What else do we need to do?
ROXY *Notices Charee.*	Oh you—ALL—have done enough. The black couch throw is just the last touch. I kinda like it.
LUCY *Donatelli enters.* *Lucy and Charee* *bump into him as* *they exit.* *With Charee.* *Exit.*	I thought you'd like black. Goodbye, Mr. Donatelli.
DONATELLI	The room looks pretty good for a broom closet—oh, ah, goodbye.
To Roxy.	That's an odd partnership for you.
ROXY	Whatever. You're the one who made me work with her. It's like a habit now. But I feel like we're on different planets, man. In different solar systems.
DONATELLI	No science talk now. This is drama!
ROXY	Thank you very much. I got everything you wanted but a bigger room.

DONATELLI Cool. How did you manage that?
Points to stuff.

ROXY We … DID it.

DONATELLI Oh, teamwork. Excellent.

ROXY But I still don't like Lucy or her Shadows.

Donatelli waves his hand and motions for her NOT to talk.
I know, I know. You're always telling us—tell the person, not you. Whatever!

DONATELLI Where is your happy little crew?

ROXY Like I'm supposed to know?

DONATELLI I see you dressed for P.E. I told you Coach could compromise.

Roxy drops what she's doing, tears the shirt and shorts off, gets her boots from behind the couch and starts putting them on. Fonso, Eddie, and Berry enter. Berry is carrying a big black plastic bag that says DKNY on the outside. He gives it to Roxy.

BERRY That girl who's related to me said you'd know what to do with this …?

ROXY Oh, the throw from Wal-Mart.

EDDIE Huh-uh, not Wal-Mart. Look at the bag.

ROXY Trust me.
Pulls out a Wal-Mart bag from the DKNY bag.
Wal-Mart. See?

FONSO	The DKNY bag was just a cover? How much trouble is that worth?
BERRY	She wouldn't let me take it into school until she emptied the DKNY sack in the back of the Jeep—dumped out rags and car wax—to hide this in. What's a throw?
ROXY *Opening the bag. Everyone helps spread the throw over the couch.*	Help me. Duh! You **throw** it!
DONATELLI	It does make the room quieter.
EDDIE	I liked it the other way.
ROXY *Hits him on the arm.*	Of course you would.
FONSO *Hits him on the arm too.*	You just aren't very hooked up, man, are you?
BERRY *All three hit him.*	I like it the other way too. Ouch. Stop the violence.
All four look at each other, then stand in front of the couch, sitting together and crossing their legs in the same direction at the same time.	
DONATELLI *Applauding.*	Bravo! OK, what do we need to teach this class?
EDDIE	A test.

FONSO	You know, that's true. If we had a test everyone had to pass, everyone would take this class seriously.
BERRY	I think a test is a good idea. I bet we can get a copy of a good test. You know, like in the teacher's textbook. And they come with a "key."
EDDIE	So … OK.

To Donatelli.

FONSO	Are there textbooks? For this class.

DONATELLI Probably.

Looks through some stuff, coming up with a big book. Yes, here's one. It feels like …
Glances through it. it's got everything in it.

Taking it.
ROXY   It **should.** Must weigh 25 pounds. This'll be
Sarcastically.   fun to haul around. 'Specially since we can't use backpacks between classes. Didn't anyone think about how easy it would be to hide a weapon in a **book**? Like this one?

The others toss it around, then give it back to Donatelli. They just sit there.

BERRY	We could go through it and Xerox off the stuff we wanted—when we wanted it …
EDDIE	Like the test.
ROXY	Are we having fun yet?
ALL	

Including Donatelli. No-o-oo! No.

Silence.

BERRY	Maybe we need to get a drama person to do this …?
FONSO	Hello? Like we'd be here—Donatelli too—if they already were going to spend the money to get a drama person to do this.
DONATELLI	It may not be **just** about money.
ROXY	What else?
DONATELLI	Truth is … teaching an art, like Theatre—or a science, like Astronomy or Chemistry—isn't a … well, science. There aren't any rules and neat formulas that you can just go out and buy and bam!—have a class that does what it's supposed to do for everyone involved: the teacher, the students, the principal, the parents, the school board, the state, everyone.

Silence.

EDDIE	I bet we could buy a better room. One with a stage … and comfy chairs.
DONATELLI	I can't argue with you there. I just know that, even *with* that, you might not put students in it and get those kids to know and understand anything about science … or theatre arts.
BERRY	Or even **like** either one.
ROXY *She gets very quiet.* *Looks at the others.*	Like with science until— —until … you know …
FONSO	Until we had to do the job for our**selves.**
EDDIE	'Cause Dr. Don't—sorry, I mean Mr.

Donatelli— wouldn't let us leave it up to him. Even though it's totally his fault.

FONSO   Totally!

ROXY   That's the point—until we did the job for ourselves.

To Donatelli.
BERRY   So that's why you asked us to help you?

DONATELLI   That's right. If learning in this class becomes everyone's job, AND mine too, then we'll have the strategy to know and understand this subject, just like science.

ROXY   Even if no one becomes a great actor—

DONATELLI   Or becomes a great scientist. Knowing about things makes your brain grow. And ... "Doncha want bigger brains?"

EDDIE   I just want Berry's.

BERRY   Take it. The theatre is how my family made money. Besides that, I sure don't know anything about theatre or drama, except that if I have to "act"—

FONSO   It'll be in a box.
High-fives with everyone.

DONATELLI   Don't **tell** me that!
Laughing harder   Just **don't** tell me that.
than anyone.   OK. Roxy thinks we're wasting time.

FONSO   What's next, Roxy? Hook us up!

ROXY	OK. Berry, take this chalk and write on the board when I tell you to.

BERRY

Starts, then looks at   All right ...
Donatelli who shrugs.

ROXY	Does he have to look at you every time? Am I chairing this thing or **not**?
DONATELLI	You are.
EDDIE	Hey, that's not fair.
FONSO	Did **you** want to be in charge?
EDDIE	No!
FONSO	Then let's get on with this.
BERRY	I'm ready.

ROXY	So—for planning purposes—each of us will represent four whole groups of students. I'm up on drama and theatre and movies. But I'm bored doing the same thing I've already done just because others don't know anything.
DONATELLI	Interested and advanced students paired with students who know nothing. No motivation.
ROXY	Berry is—
EDDIE	—Way smart in school subjects and taking tests—
BERRY	—But doesn't think knowing drama is very important to his future or life.

FONSO	And doesn't get scared of anything as much as performing in front of someone.
DONATELLI	Academically smart students unable to see the value of Theatre Arts knowledge who also see little reason for risking embarrassment in a performance.
ROXY	And, Eddie, you are—
EDDIE	—Like totally not into school. Too many rules. No boards. No freedom. Bad grades no matter what I do.
BERRY	Not always.
EDDIE	True, du-ude. True. Not **quite** always.
DONATELLI	Unmotivated students with no support for getting good grades or playing by the rules.
EDDIE	That's **me**!
ROXY	And how many kids signed up for Elective B are like you?
EDDIE	Like Wade and Bomber, for sure. Some others too.

Silence.

OK, Fonso, what about you? 'Cause **I'm** not going to explain what kind of student you are.

BERRY	Me neither.
ROXY	I don't think I would, even if I wanted to.
FONSO	I'll be all the **other** students.

Very emotional.

No labels. OK?

ROXY	OK with me.

Looks at Donatelli.

DONATELLI You'd be ... "Miscellaneous Students" then?
*Fonso doesn't say
anything or look up.*

ROXY   That's OK, isn't it?

DONATELLI Miscellaneous is just a label for a category
so we can have four, since that's how many
Roxy wants to represent.

FONSO   Oh, I thought "miscellaneous" was some kind
of retarded **special** group.

EDDIE   That's how my dad sorts the wash; everything's
miscellaneous. My mom says that makes all
our clothes have the same color—

ALL   Miscellaneous.

ROXY   Maybe putting names and labels on kinds of
students isn't a very good idea. Maybe there
are just a couple of things that all kids—

BERRY   Students—

ROXY   Students need. Like motivation.

EDDIE   People to nag you.

BERRY   Easier ways to do the class.

FONSO   For the class to be interesting.

DONATELLI Students who want to be there.

ROXY   Like Berry ...

DONATELLI ... In Science. But in this class, **students,**
like you.

ROXY   Whatever!

*Stares at him, then
at the others.
To Donatelli.*

OK. OK, OK. I want to be in this class now.
Happy?

DONATELLI Yes, thank you.

BERRY How does it feel, Roxy?

*She glares at him
and throws her
T-shirt at him.*

I meant, OK, Roxy, what's next?

Silence.

DONATELLI What should students know at the end of this
term? How do they get to know it? How will
you show the principal, parents, and the
students that they know it?

BERRY How will students be **graded**?

ROXY I know. Really I do. I just don't know how to
say it—put it all into words.

BERRY I get that way a lot.
FONSO When you're asleep?

BERRY No.

EDDIE I thought teaching was a lot easier than this.

FONSO And **we're** trying to help. When those jocks
get back here tomorrow—

ROXY And Lucy and her backup singers—

BERRY And all those skater kids who will just drop out
after the second day—

EDDIE Hey, little bro … back off, even if it **is** true.

FONSO	And what about the kids we don't even know about that don't speak English very well and others that don't know how to read English?
ROXY	This is **way** more than four categories.
DONATELLI	Maybe the whole **class** should help ...?
BERRY	Sounds messy to me. But we could make a few choices—like doing a play and reading the textbook—and then ask the rest of the class what they think about everything. A questionnaire, you know ...
FONSO	They won't take it seriously.
EDDIE	How come **we** are?
ROXY	Donatelli asked us to.

P.A. squawks.

P.A. VOICE	Mr. Donatelli. Mr. Donatelli. Please meet Assistant Principal Stone in the Cafeteria Annex immediately.
DONATELLI	Gotta go. Looks like registration for Elective B went up. I bet Third Period just got moved back to the Cafeteria Annex.
ROXY	What about the room?
EDDIE	I don't think it can be moved.

Leaving.

DONATELLI	Welcome to teaching. Meet me in the cafeteria, before Advisory, tomorrow morning ... You too, Eddie. Think Pop Tarts and Shakespeare. This just might be fun!

Exits.

*They all watch
Mr. D leave. The
P.A. comes back on.*

P.A. VOICE Mr. Donatelli, meet Mr. Stone in the Cafeteria
Annex right away. Elective B has to be
rescheduled there. Mr. Donatelli, meet
Mr. Stone in the Cafeteria Annex.

*Roxy starts putting
stuff on the sofa. Then
she begins sliding it
toward the door.*

**THE
OTHERS** Roxy, what are you **doing**?

ROXY Help me. We're taking the couch with us.

EDDIE Where?

ROXY Where it belongs—in our Third Period!

*They slide the couch
out. The room is left
empty for a few
seconds.*

Blackout.

aha! Process, Inc.
(800) 424-9484

A Play in One Act
Double Trouble
Cheryl E. Davis

[Remember, all main characters can be developed as boys or girls using the alternative names listed to suit the composition of the group doing the play. Please adjust the pronoun references for each character throughout the text when these changes are made.]

BERRY [BERRY]	... not a cool dresser
EDDIE [EDY]	... surfer dude or dudette
FONSO [ALLY]	... cool, "the bomb" (to kids, not parents or teachers)
ROXY [ROCKY]	... whatever ... Harley look to hip hop
MR. DONATELLI	... Science teacher
LUCY, TYRA, & CHAREE	... cheerleaders
MATTHEW, LUKE, JOHN, & MICHAEL	... jocks
NINE OTHERS	... representatives of other school groups: nerds, freaks, preppies, et al.

aha! Process, Inc.
(800) 424-9484

[Each cast/class will have to carefully decide and dress for this scene to make the point.]

THE SETTING

The main characters are seated as students from different groups enter, crowd in, look around, and sit down, all trying to sit or stand in the same area near the door until Donatelli can hardly be seen. There is a huge bunch of students milling around. Those entering are a microcosm of how different groups identify themselves in school.

BLACKOUT!

Flashlights zoom like lightning around the darkened space preceding the voices. The voices belong to the foursome.

VOICE 1	Double, double
ALL	Toil and trouble!
VOICE 1	Fire burn, and cauldron bubble.
ALL	Toil and trouble! … Now the charm's wound up!

A flashlight comes on.

DONATELLI

Holding a flashlight on his face. In a Dracula voice.

Dr-r-rama-a! "The Art of Make-Believe." Theatre: T-H-E-A-T-R-E, not "E-R." Live actors holding a mirror to Life in front of a Live audience, charming them … Or-r-r— Live actors captured in the mirror of a camera's lens … to charm an audience again and again.

Flashlights off. From the dark.

FONSO	Ladies and gentlemen, live from the Cafeteria Annex:
ROXY	Featuring the ever-popular Science teacher, Mr. Donatelli, in his new role as Theatre Arts professore.

Classroom lights up.

FONSO	Welcome to "An Introduction to Theatre Arts"!

*The four **clap** until everyone else does. Mr. D bows.*

DONATELLI	Thank you. Thank you.
LUKE	Good thing you didn't try to sell tickets to **this** show.

The class laughs, and a few overreact until Fonso steps toward the show-offs, who stop right away.

DONATELLI	OK. The first thing this show is going to have ... is a **test.**

Starts passing out paper and pencils. Everyone gets upset.

Calm down. You already know the answers. You just don't know **what** you know—YET!

Some moaning and groaning still.

JOHN	This is supposed to be ... ah, an **easy** class. No homework or tests, you know?
LUCY	Surprise tests are also against district policy.

aha! Process, Inc.
(800) 424-9484

To Lucy.

    DONATELLI Thank you, Lucy.

    EDDIE Surprise! Surprise!

    DONATELLI Ready?

Everyone complains and calls out, "Wait!" Put your name in the right-hand corner. No. 1. Write the question down, please. I'll repeat each one three times.

    ROXY So no one has to have it repeated.

    DONATELLI And leave room on your paper after each question to write the answer.

To Roxy. Here, you read the questions.

    EDDIE Three times?

    FONSO So no one has to have 'em repeated.

Donatelli sits back at the desk in the middle of most of the students.

    ROXY

Taking the papers, roughly. Reading very quickly. Then slowing. No. 1. What is the back of a stage called? What … is the back … of a stage … called?

    ALL We got it, OK?

    ROXY OK. No. 2. What is the **front** of a stage called?

    LUCY Everyone knows this.

    CHAREE Not me.

aha! Process, Inc.
(800) 424-9484

EDDIE	Me neither.
ROXY	Knock it off.
DONATELLI	Please.
ROXY	Whatever? Please knock it off. No. 3. What is left and right and center on a stage?
FONSO	Again.
ROXY	What is left and right—
EDDIE	Wait. Roxy, this doesn't make any sense.
ROXY *Looks at the rest.*	Just copy it. You can figure it out later. You guys copy it too. You too Lucy.
LUCY	What are you, the **teacher**?
ROXY	Not exactly. And **center** on a stage? No. 4. Leave some room to write the answers.
TYRA & CHAREE	Wa-it! … right and center on a stage.
ROXY	Copy Lucy's. No. 4. Ready? Why do you need to know stage positions?
EDDIE *Singing, Mouseketeer style …*	Why? Because we love to.
FONSO	Eddie, chill.
ROXY	Got it? No. 5.
CHAREE	How many of these **are** there?

DONATELLI
Without looking up. A hundred.

CHAREE Fine.

ROXY Fine. 5. What are three differences between acting and reading?
To Donatelli. **I** don't get **this** one.

EDDIE I wrote this one. It's mine.

ROXY Oh. No wonder. What are the differences between acting and reading? Everyone OK to go on?

Mumbling agreement. No. 6. What is the biggest problem when you are performing? Does anyone need seconds? OK. No. 7. What does "better" mean?

LUCY This is getting seriously stupid now …

FONSO No, that's part of the answer to No. 6.

BERRY Whatever. Let's get **on** with this.

Sarcastically.
LUCY Oo-oo!
To Berry. He speaks.

ROXY Cut it out, Lucy. OK, 8. No. 8.

BERRY I would like to say that I don't get BETTER either.

ROXY No. 8, please! What does the word FREEZE! mean to this class?

BERRY That's a science term.

DONATELLI Not originally.

| ROXY | Excuse me? 9. Ready? |

More mumbling and grumbling.

| LUKE | I don't think we can live through a hundred of these. |

Groaning.

| ROXY | Me neither ... No. 9: What are 10 reasons why Shakespeare is important to studying Theatre Arts? S-h-a-k-e-s-p-e-a-r-e ... "Shake a spear" ... Get it? |

Groaning. | Whatever!

| EDDIE | Ten? Only 90 left. I'm dead. |

Everyone else agrees.

| ROXY | That was No. 9. You need 10 answers, duh? What are 10 reasons why Shakespeare is important to studying theatre? And question No. 10— |

| BERRY | Should we leave 10 lines after this question? |

| LUKE | To 9 or 10? |

| ROXY | To question No. 9, ye-es! Duh? |

| EDDIE | Good question, Berry Boy. |

| ROXY | OK, OK. 10. What are the most common stage directions, and what do they mean? |

Groaning and many calling out, "Wait!" | What ... are ... the most common ... the ... most ... common ... stage ... directions ... and what do they mean? OK.

Much groaning. | And ... what ... do ... they ... mean?

aha! Process, Inc.
(800) 424-9484

FONSO	We need it again.
ROXY	Good grief!
BERRY	You said you'd read it three times …
ROXY	Whatever. WHAT … ARE … THE … MOST … COMMON (I can't do this 90 more times) … MOST COMMON … STAGE … DIRECTIONS … AND … WHAT … DO … THEY … MEAN?

From his desk.

DONATELLI	Thanks, Roxy. That's enough for now.
EVERYONE	Yea!!!!

Momentary pandemonium.

DONATELLI	Fonso? Collect all the tests, please.

No one moves, except Mr. D.

ROXY	They aren't finished … answering them …

Class agrees, loudly.

DONATELLI	I only asked everyone to **copy** the questions. Fonso?

LUKE, EDDIE, & OTHERS	He wants his stupid questions back. Why? Don't ask, just pass. Let me see your ninth question.

Several students grab their papers back, while others work frantically, copying and writing. Eddie hums the Jeopardy! *song. Fonso finally gets them collected.*

Ad-lib.

aha! Process, Inc.
(800) 424-9484

*Class reassembles
during all this
commotion, with
Mr. D handing out
flashlights and
moving people
against the sides.
He sits down, almost
offstage; his back is
to the audience.*

DONATELLI	Let's start again. Ready?
BERRY	What about the **test**?
LUCY & ROXY	Sha-ah-ahup, Berry.
DONATELLI	We can start there—
OTHERS	No-oooo!
DONATELLI	Or … we can go back to Macbeth.
CHAREE	I'm hungry; this is great.
LUCY	Beth! Mac-BETH, not MAC-Donald's.
ROXY	A guy—
BERRY	King guy. Not a hamburger.
CHAREE	I knew that.
LUKE, TYRA, & EDDIE	I'd like a Big Mac.
ROXY & LUCY	Get over it!

aha! Process, Inc.
(800) 424-9484

EDDIE
Sarcastically.   Sorr-rry!

DONATELLI From the top then.
He hands out scripts.

    ROXY   He means, Go back to the beginning.

DONATELLI Lucy, Roxy, Charee, and Tyra put one script on
this music stand—

Puts it in the middle
of them. There is   Join hands.
a long pause.   You are conjuring a spell.

    FONSO   It also says here that they are the weird sisters.
Laughter and
high-fives.

    BERRY   And ugly! Ugly hags!
Roxy pushes
Berry over; he   Hey!
sprawls on the floor.

DONATELLI The play is 400 years old, and it's set several
hundred years before that. Think of the
witches, the sisters, as omens.

    EDDIE   Play?

    BERRY   MACBETH.

DONATELLI "Weird and ugly" didn't just refer to how
people looked, but to the kind of knowledge
they possessed, compared with the everyday
person. These creatures—

    THREE
    JOCKS   No kidding!
*Lucy pushes **them***
over.

DONATELLI —Set the stage for a play about greed and ambition and murder.

EDDIE   Cool! I've seen this.

ROXY   "Macbeth" is a play written by William Shakespeare. When have you seen a stage play by anyone?

EDDIE   Oh, I thought it was a movie.

DONATELLI It could have been a movie plot. Shakespeare's plots show up in a lot of movies and TV shows and modern plays.

BERRY   A 400-year-old movie? I don't think so.

CLASS   We agree with Berry.

DONATELLI Ladies, join hands. And circle the music stand
Ignoring everyone ... saying the lines as you go.

ROXY   Don't we need to know who the first witch is?

CLASS   Speak for yourself, Roxy.

DONATELLI Say the lines in unison and pretend to be evil.

They just stand still.

LUCY   The words. We all say the words **together,** at the same time. And some of us don't have to **pretend** to be evil.

CLASS   OO-oo-oo.

ROXY   Bite your tongue, Lucy.

DONATELLI We'll do one run-through, and then we'll practice with the lights and sound.

aha! Process, Inc.
(800) 424-9484

BERRY   Who's doing sound?

DONATELLI   All of you. You three: Go "whooosh, whoosh."
Points to 3-4   More "ooosh." Yes. And you, make a light
students ... in each hissing sound. (H)'ssssssssss,ss,ssss, ... lightly
direction ...   sssss,s,ss, again. Louder and then quieter, all
                 of you, with the words. The rest of you: Lightly
                 snap your fingers. That's it ... louder when
                 there's no dialogue—

FONSO   —"Talking by the weirdos."

DONATELLI   Talking by weirdos. Sisters. Weird sisters.
                 Or brothers. It doesn't have anything to do
                 with your neighborhood ... or your soul
                 brothers or sisters.

Class starts
mumbling.   It's a sisterhood of looks, knowledge, and
                 deeds, not race. It's 400 years old—in England.

EDDIE   Oh yeah, England—up past New York City.

ROXY   That's NEW England, Eddie.

DONATELLI
Smiles.   Way, way up past and to the right of the
                 Atlantic Ocean ...

Back on focus. Lightly snap your fingers. Good. Berry, you
                 turn the light switch off when I tell you to.
                 Ladies, have you got your lines down?

ROXY   He means us. We sort of have them down.

DONATELLI   OK, everyone practice what you're going to do.
Pause.   Quietly. Practice to yourself. Ignore everyone
                 else. Just do what I told you.

*There is general
commotion and
buzzing: lines and
noises and flashes
for a minute.*
OK. Ready. Ladies, join hands. Wait for lights. Berry.

*Class lights go out.
Flashlights come up
on the four girlz' faces.
The whooshing, then
hissing, then rain-like
snapping gets very
loud, then fades.*

THE GIRLZ Double! Double. Toil and trouble.
Fire burn and cauldron bubble.

*They pause. The
background noise
gets very loud, then
softens with the lines.*
When shall we three meet again
In thunder, lightning, or in rain?
When the hurly burly's done,
When the battle's lost and won.
A drum …

Pause.

LUCY   I said, "A drum?"
Lights come back up.

EDDIE   Way to break character, Lucy!

DONATELLI We **do** need a drum … soon.

ROXY   She read it wrong.

TYRA   We weren't there yet.

LUCY   Tyra!

TYRA	Well, we **weren't,** and it was getting really good.
DONATELLI	It **was** good.
FONSO	If it was supposed to be weird—and creepy—it was great.
DONATELLI	What does that make you expect next?
JOCKS & EDDIE	Something more weird. Weirder, like totally weird.
EDDIE	Who knows what … I didn't get what the words meant. I know what double and trouble mean. But what's burly?
CHAREE	Like a total babe magnet.
TYRA	It reads "Hurly Burly."
CHAREE	OK, a babe magnet who's throwing up.
ROXY, LUCY, & BERRY	Not!!
DONATELLI	Hurly burly's a storm—or what a storm over water is like.
FONSO	It's a ride too. At Six Flags.
EDDIE	It's also totally what you do when your board hits a pothole … or a wave … sideways.

There is some high-fiving.

	You get over wanting to hurl. And I thought a cauldron was a fancy trick board.
ROXY	It's a big pot, you freak.

aha! Process, Inc.
(800) 424-9484

JOCKS	Why are they riding in a pot?
LUCY	They're throwing things **into** the pot.
TYRA	And dancing around it.
BERRY	While a storm is going on.
CHAREE	Very, very weird. They got a pot. And then they want a drum?
ROXY	They hear a drum.
LUCY & FONSO	From somewhere else. Not the pot.
LUCY & ROXY	No, from, from …
DONATELLI	From offstage.
GIRLZ	Uh-huh.
DONATELLI	The sound pulls our attention off the stage and toward the next action … the next character.
FONSO	I'll be the drummer. How many times?

DONATELLI Really fast. Like this.

Hits hands on a desk,
Slap. Slap, slap-slap. Pause in between. **Again** and **again.**
Everyone does the
drumming. They all
look at scripts.

FONSO Oh, Macbeth is coming.

LUCY Duh! A drum, a drum, Macbeth doth come.
Everyone looks So these people lisp?
puzzled. You know, DOTH. Macbeth do**th** come.

aha! Process, Inc.
(800) 424-9484

ROXY	It's just old-fashioned English for "does."
LUCY	And **you** are **right,** because …
DONATELLI	… Because she **IS.** Shakespeare wrote in Elizabethan English. It's not Old English, which sounds like German. And it's not Middle English, which is different enough from modern English that it needs to be translated. The King James Version of the Bible is in Elizabethan English, which also sometimes needs translation.
BERRY *Everyone stares at him.*	That explains the "Verilys" … You know, "Verily, verily an angel brought forth a babe and wrapped him in swaddling clothes."
ROXY	**Mary** brought forth the babe.
FONSO	Whatever … It's 400-year-old English.
DONATELLI	Let's take it from the top now.
LUCY	He means—
THE CLASS	From the beginning!
DONATELLI	Practice, everyone.

The rest of the class returns to the noisy but orderly chaos of practicing. Donatelli steps out of working with the ladies, picks up a script, and gives it to Roxy, who pulls away from the others.

aha! Process, Inc.
(800) 424-9484

She slips into a big team jacket as she pulls a chair out (center), turns, and sits with her back to the audience. The practice noise increases, but it sounds better. Each group is focused and intense.

*At some point the class noise goes silent, and the class is seen in **pantomime**. We only **hear Roxy**. She pretends to be holding a letter.*

ROXY
With feeling and meaning.

They met me on the day of success. They have more than mortal knowledge. When I went to question them further, they vanished. While I stood rapt in wonder, a messenger from the king hailed me as "Thane of Cawdor," by which title these weird sisters had saluted me. This I write to thee, my dearest wife, that thou mayest rejoice at what greatness is promised thee. Farewell.

She puts the paper down.

To herself.

Gel. No glaw. Mis. Caw! Cow. Door. Ee-oo! Elizabethan English is so full of stupid words.

Continuing ... turning halfway around.

Macbeth. Thou art and thou shalt be king as thou wast promised. Yet I do fear thy nature.

*Fonso and Berry turn quietly and stand, listening. The rest turn and listen as Roxy turns all the way around. **As she finishes, the others applaud, slowly at first, then with respect and gusto.***

It is too full of the milk of human kindness to catch the nearest way. Hurry hither, that I may pour my spirits in thine ear and chastise with my tongue all that impedes thee from the golden crown.

How long have you been listening?

BERRY   Since "the milk of human kindness" …

FONSO   Who are you supposed to be?

ROXY   Lady Macbeth.

EDDIE   Oh, like the Queen.

DONATELLI Not yet. Macbeth isn't the king **yet** either.

EDDIE   Of Scotland?

FONSO &
BERRY   Yes.

DONATELLI Way, **way** up past New York City.

EDDIE   I know where England is now. Kinda.

DONATELLI Well, Scotland's a little piece of land north of England, facing into the North Sea. Scotland was always being invaded, even by the English.

ROXY   And by Macbeth.

DONATELLI He does take over the kingdom.

FONSO   And it's not his.

aha! Process, Inc.
(800) 424-9484

BERRY	But the witches tell him to. Sort of. Well, I guess they don't exactly order him to kill King Duncan.
FONSO	But Macbeth **thinks** they do.
ROXY	So does Lady Macbeth. It's like if the weirdos said it, then killing was OK. To make a prophecy come true ... anything was OK.
BERRY	Laws were different back then.
ROXY	People weren't. Famous people, rich people still act like they're supposed to get things just because someone tells them to want them or they just wanted them anyway. And they can afford to get whatever they want.
FONSO	It's not just true for the famous or the rich. Where I live ... there are people—guys—who rule their neighborhood, just like it was Scotland.
ROXY	And the girls act like Lady Macbeth queens.
EDDIE	Who is like the witches?
FONSO	TV. Teachers. Parents ... always telling us what's OK to want. And some guys just think if they're the strongest, then God is on their side, because they wear crosses and rosaries.
DONATELLI	Or the Devil is on their side.
FONSO	For a fact, man. Shakespeare nails it. Except Shakespeare is really hard to read. I've never read anything so many times and still couldn't get it. Well, besides History.

ROXY   And every time I think I get it, another word
              jumps up that is totally not anything—
              especially not English—to me.

BERRY   Modern English.
FONSO   Except when we start to put it together, giving
              parts out and saying things out loud—it starts
              to make sense, even when I don't get all the
              words exactly.

DONATELLI   Drama: "2 Points." Ignorance: "Zero."

EDDIE   So, Mr. D ... 'Snext?

*The others sit
around the edge of
the classroom.*

DONATELLI   Making it better.

CLASS
Upset. Mumbling.

FONSO   I thought you said we **were** good.

DONATELLI   I did. You are.

Angry.
BERRY   I don't get it. Then why do we want to
              get better?

ROXY   This is starting to sound like every other
Losing her cool. class. There's always a trick. Now we have to
              be **better.** What a rip! This way you don't
              have to give everyone who is good an **A.** This
              is just the same ol', same ol'.

*The class gets
agitated too.*

DONATELLI   Lucy, what is district policy on this?

LUCY *Sputtering and* *off guard.*	On what? Only giving **A**'s to the kids who can do better?
DONATELLI	Yes.
LUCY & **ROXY**	That's **not** what you said.
DONATELLI	I said, The next thing we're going to do is learn how to make what we're doing—THIS PLAY—better. I did NOT say, You (any of you) were "bad" or awful. Or not getting an **A.** "Making it better"is the next part of studying. Let's agree on what "better" means. Ready? It means **not stopping.** NOT TELLING YOUR-SELF THAT "YOU'RE DONE NOW" when it's going well. In fact, "better" means a performance or idea was good—good enough to find a way to make it even "better."
CLASS *Deflated.*	Oh.
ROXY *Irritated.*	It just means ... "better"?
EDDIE	Duh?
BERRY	This **is** just like Science class.
LUCY	You think everything is like Science.
BERRY *Opens his mouth.* *Then closes it.*	You think everything is like **cheer**leading. So **better** ... just means better.
FONSO	That's what the man said.

DONATELLI One way to get better is to speak the same
He clears a wide language as what you're studying.
area in front of In this case … stage language.
the chalkboard.
Draws a trapezoid
on the board, gives
Fonso and Eddie
masking tape, and
they make the same
shape, larger, on the
floor.

LUCY &
ROXY
Glare at each other
but end up answering
together. I know what that is.

DONATELLI OK?

LUCY A stage.

Irritated.
ROXY The basic stage shape.
Realizes she is
coming on too strong. I'm a little hyper, OK? It's a stage …

EDDIE … Where you act from.

DONATELLI Is the stage real?

At the same time.
LUCY &
ROXY Yes.

BERRY No.

EDDIE &
LUKE Yes.

LUCY &	
ROXY	No? Yes. What do you mean?
DONATELLI	If I erase the board and lift the tape, will there still be a "stage" here?

At the same time.

CLASS	YES. NO. No. Yes.

Silence.

ROXY
Whispering to Lucy first. They agree and come forward. Lifting the tape.   If we take the tape ... up ...

EDDIE &	
FONSO	Hey! Stop—
LUCY	But stand here ... and think of this space ... as

Joining in.

ROXY	... The stage. The place we know we want the audience to see us in.
LUCY	With or with**out** the tape or the drawing. This is where the action and lines are seen and heard.
BERRY	The stage becomes like the world we live in.

ROXY
Stepping back, outside the tape.   And this is OFFstage.

EDDIE
Jumping to Lucy.   ONstage.
Jumping to Roxy.   OFFstage. On. Off. Off. On. Still ON.
Roxy chases him off.   Almost off. **Way** off.

ROXY
Walks in front
of Lucy,   And this is
stands close
to audience.   DOWNstage.

LUCY
Goes farther back.   And back here is UPstage.

ROXY   Eddie?

EDDIE
Runs, then stops,
jumps, back   UP?
and forth.   Down. Up. Down. Oops, off, now on. Up.
     Now down.

Class claps.

BERRY   So why isn't it BACKstage and FRONTstage?

LUCY   HELLO? It just isn't.

ROXY   Well, backstage is where you get ready to go
     onstage. And you come ON from OFFstage.

FONSO   I'm gettin' dizzy.

To Donatelli.
ROXY   Help, please.

LUCY   I'm confused now.

DONATELLI On and off: just names for things.
     You know, labels? For places on the stage.
     And movements on the stage.
     Start with the beginning of things.

All nod as he moves
onstage.   Like brake pedals on a bike.
     If you pedal to brake a bike and you have more
     than one speed …

JOCKS *All high-five.*	You will crash! You will **not** stop.
DONATELLI	Stopping takes—
EDDIE & BERRY, PLUS THREE JOCKS	Brake pads!
DONATELLI	And you don't use the pedals, you use the—
EDDIE	Gearshift … on the handlebars.
GIRLZ	YOU do. We use the hand brakes below the gearshift on the handlebars.
EDDIE	I knew that.
JOCKS	Duh?
DONATELLI	In the olden days—
FONSO	Back then, or if you have a classic bike—
EDDIE	A Pee Wee Herman bike—
DONATELLI	You stepped back on the pedal to brake.
ROXY	OK, but a stage is **not** a bike.
LUCY *Tyra, Charee, and Lucy high-five. Roxy joins with them … looks uncomfortable, then is able to enjoy the joke on herself. To Roxy. Class claps.*	Let's hear it for Genius Woman! Genius Woman! But the stage, like a bike, has names for its

different places and parts. OK, so why is back
… **up** and front … **down**?

DONATELLI

*Donatelli picks up
the music stand.
Class mumbles.*

*Tilting it to show
what he is
saying.*

Geography. And the need to see.
Go back 3,000 or so years. The Greeks lived
in a warm climate. Their lands were hilly.
The bottoms of hills made perfect stages.
When the Romans took over, it was the same
climate and terrain—

BERRY   Geography. Sit on the hill to watch a play.

EDDIE   Cool.

DONATELLI   Actually, theatre … plays … started as dances.
And when plays went north where it rained and
snowed, there was no climate or natural place
for a stage or an audience.

BERRY   Then what?

DONATELLI   Nothing. For a long time. Except for Bible
stories or local stories played out in churches in
front of the parishioners, but there weren't any
theatres either. Not yet.

ROXY   The Dark Ages, huh?

BERRY   I was going to say that.

LUCY   Consider it said, Berry.

FONSO   Dark Ages?

DONATELLI Most of the first millennium from Jesus' birth. Bad weather. Christianity tries to replace the barbarians who tried to replace Roman rule. Then Crusades. Plagues. It's a history no one thinks is very relevant to us.

TYRA Relevant?

LUCY Important, you know. Interesting. Duh? So why were they called **dark**?

DONATELLI Several reasons. Stormy, cloudy. Few could read. And there wasn't any time if you **could** read. Books, even learning—especially learning anything new—was considered evil. There were no printing presses or scanners. The printed word was monks copying books, using quill pens and ink, hour after hour, day after day, in monasteries.

Rich or poor, you spent what time you lived … around 20 to 30 years … in one 10-mile radius.

CHAREE Your whole life in practically one block. Ee-oo.

EDDIE No video games!

ROXY No electricity, man.

FONSO No running water. No plumbing. No toilets.

LUCY Eee-ooo!

BERRY No gunpowder. No guns. A plow and a knife.

DONATELLI No literature. No art. Except in decorating things everyone needed.

BERRY Like swords and churches and pottery.

ROXY   No theatre. Except some plays in churches.

DONATELLI   Which moved to carts and could be driven from church to church or driven to marketplaces and courtyards when there were no churches.

FONSO   And the carts could be the stages!

DONATELLI   Along with the markets and courtyards.
*High-fives Fonso and
then everyone does.*

EDDIE   Portable hills. Only switched around.

ROXY   Huh?

EDDIE   Make the cart like a valley floor and put a roof over it ... for when it rains—

BERRY   A trailer.

DONATELLI   Sort of. At any rate, the audience is now below the stage, except when the cart parks at a castle.

ROXY   Then all that the rich people (and their servants) have to do is sit in their windows and look out—at the cart or the courtyard.

LUCY   The stage is born.

DONATELLI   Well, when they finally came to building theatres and performing plays for fun, about Shakespeare's time, the buildings imitated a courtyard with a church altar at the back, and that became the stage. And only the stage had a roof, and the theatre roof was open ... to—

EDDIE   —To let the world in.

BERRY   And light.

aha! Process, Inc.
(800) 424-9484

FONSO At night?

DONATELLI Daytime. There wouldn't be electric lights for another 300 years. By Shakespeare's time plays were performed in theatres in the day time, after people went to market. Theatres could pretend to be anyplace, anytime in the world. But actually **seeing** them took the sun, the daytime.

EDDIE Awesome! Like the Globe Theatre, huh?

ROXY How did you know that?

LUCY He was abducted by aliens. They told him.

CHAREE Know what?

TYRA
To Charee. He had a globe.

ROXY The Globe was the name of Shakespeare's Theatre.

LUCY Which had an open roof to let the sunlight in …

FONSO Because they saw the plays in the daytime …

TYRA &
CHAREE Because the people had just gone shopping in the market …

JOCKS Because nothing had been invented like fridges to keep the food fresh.

EDDIE Where did they keep their food?

DONATELLI In their pockets, while they were standing in front of the stage. Which meant if they didn't like the show or the actors, they would take out some food—eggs, tomatoes—and throw it at the actors.

CLASS Cool!

ROXY Back in those days food fights also entertained the rich who were sitting in seats above the crowd of common people.

DONATELLI Which the common people couldn't see. So ... getting back to the point about why stages are up and down instead of back and front ... As time went on, if they raised the back of the stage, tilted it up, a little—

Tilts the music stand down to illustrate.

EDDIE The people standing could see what was on the stage better.

ROXY And the front, by the audience, would be DOWN!

LUCY The front is DOWN.

FONSO The back is UP.

DONATELLI OK, it gets better.

CLASS

Mumbling. Oh no, "better." WORD!
Groaning.

DONATELLI With actors and writers, and plays and stages, came directors ... who sat in the audience, facing—

CLASS DOWNstage!! The front!

aha! Process, Inc.
(800) 424-9484

DONATELLI

Walks the stage as he speaks.

So they gave names to each part of the stage— from the actor's position on the stage. So the director could tell them where to move and stand without having to get up on stage and show them all the time, if they got confused. That gives us: nine basic places on the stage. Upstage center. Center stage—the middle, like in basketball.

Moves where he speaks.

CLASS

Just like basketball! Go, Mr. D!

DONATELLI

Some of cast follow behind him. The rest sit politely on the floor, backs to audience, in front of Mr. D who goes back to center stage.

Downstage center. Now sit in front of me, as much as possible. Watch. If I say the word "stage," what do I mean? Downstage right. Downstage center. Downstage left.

Stage center ...
Stage right. Stage left. Now, upstage center. Upstage right. Stage center. Upstage left. Now, if I skip center, and I'm sitting out there where you are, telling "me" to skip center ... Then I say—to me on the stage—

He goes upstage right.

"Cross down left."

The class points downstage left.

And I go ... downstage left. Ta-daa!

The students who are improvising his moves all bump into him in several Three Stooges crashes. There is applause. Then ...

(The following section is the final scene. But it also can be separated from its Berrytale *and performed as a Readers' Theatre presentation.)*

Two groups form on stage—backs to the audience, like performing rings—all practicing Donatelli's stage directions ... walking them out on pretend stages. The cast gets lost in the middle of the groups practicing.

The actors freeze. Lights dim. The nine places on stage are repeated in unison. Then they freeze again, momentarily.

The groups turn toward the audience, slowly. Some start making the "storm" sounds from the beginning scene, as background, while the rest speak together in a Readers' Theatre format. The following allows the class members in the Berrytale, *as well as the students reading it, to put together everything they have learned about drama into a performance.*

'Hurly Burly'

A Readers' Theatre Presentation
from
MACBETH

by William Shakespeare
(arranged by Cheryl E. Davis)

CHARACTERS *
The entire class is divided as ...

STORM *{Sounds when needed or desired—finger clicking, rubbing, whooshing—could be a set group, or each of the speaking groups could take turns ... AND these sounds also could make a RAP out of this presentation.}*

aha! Process, Inc.
(800) 424-9484

GROUP   *{Always more than one speaker. The group is the conscience, chorus, and feelings of the characters, audience, and author. There could be more than one group.}*

ROXY as
VOICE 1   *{Always one speaker. These are the*

LUCY as
VOICE 2   *individual voices of the*

TYRA as
VOICE 3   *characters—witches/omens,*
              Macbeth, Lady Macbeth, et al.}

* Or as few as four parts could be used if one person makes storm sounds and joins with each of the three "voices" to read together as one group.

ALL	All hail, Macbeth!
GROUP	Double, double.
ALL	All hail, thane of Glamis (GLAWMZ)!
GROUP	All hail, thane of Cawdor (KAWdoor)!
GROUP	Toil and trouble!

Whenever this phrase is spoken, STORM joins in.

STORM	…
VOICE 1	Thou shalt be king hereafter.
ALL	Double …
GROUP	Trouble!
VOICE 2	Your face, Macbeth, is a book

VOICE 3	Where people may read your thoughts ...
GROUP	Toil and trouble.
STORM	...
VOICE 1	Look like the innocent flower
VOICE 2	But be the serpent under it ...
ALL	Double, double toil and trouble. Fire burn, and cauldron bubble.

Circling an imaginary pot as omens and witches.

STORM	...
VOICE 3	'Tis time!
VOICE 1	'Twere best to do it quickly!
ALL	Thou shalt be king hereafter!
VOICE 2	TOMORROW.
VOICE 3	'Tis time!

Pause.

ALL	AND TOMORROW ...
GROUP	AND TOMORROW CREEPS IN THIS PETTY PACE.

Thrice the black cat hath mew'd.

Screaming!
Screaming!

Thrice the hedgehog whined.

aha! Process, Inc.
(800) 424-9484

VOICE 1	Her eyes …
Pause.	… are open.
VOICE 2	But her senses …
Pause.	… are shut.
ALL BUT VOICE 1	Look, how she rubs her hands.

In agony.

VOICE 1	YET HERE'S A SPOT! OUT, DAMNED SPOT! OUT, I SAY.

Crying.

WILL THESE HANDS NEVER BE CLEAN?

Sadly, fearfully.

GROUP	We have heard … what we … should not!
ALL	Double, double toil and trouble.
STORM	…
GROUP	AND TOMORROW CREEPS IN THIS PETTY PACE
VOICE 3	FROM DAY TO DAY, TO THE LAST SYLLABLE OF RECORDED TIME.
VOICE 2	'Tis time!
VOICE 1	'Tis time!
GROUP	AND ALL OUR YESTERDAYS HAVE LIGHTED FOOLS THE WAY TO DUSTY DEATH.

Circling the cauldron … totally freaking.

VOICE 1	Round about the cauldron go.
VOICE 2	In the poisoned entrails throw.
GROUP	… False face must hide what the false heart doth know.
VOICE 3	Double, double toil and trouble.
STORM	…
ALL	Fire burn, and cauldron bubble!

Shouting.

GROUP	OUT, OUT BRIEF CANDLE!
VOICE 1	Fillet of fenny snake
VOICE 2	In the cauldron,
VOICE 3	Boil and bake!
VOICE 1	Eye of newt,
GROUP	DOUBLE, DOUBLE!
VOICE 2	And toe of frog,
GROUP	TOIL AND TROUBLE!
STORM	…
VOICE 3	Wool of bat
VOICE 2	And tongue of dog,
VOICE 1	Adder's fork
VOICE 2	And blind-worm's sting,

VOICE 3	Lizard's leg and owlet's wing,
VOICE 1	For a charm of powerful trouble—
GROUP	DOUBLE, DOUBLE TOIL AND TROUBLE!
STORM	…
VOICES 1 & 2	… Broth boil!
VOICES 2 & 3	Broth bubble!
ALL	Double, double toil and trouble, Fire burn, and cauldron bubble.
GROUP	LIFE'S BUT A WALKING SHADOW, A POOR PLAYER …
ALL	When shall we three meet again?
GROUP	A POOR PLAYER THAT STRUTS AND FRETS HIS HOUR UPON THE STAGE AND THEN IS HEARD NO MORE. Double, double toil and trouble!

Storm throughout.

STORM	…
ALL	In thunder? Lightning? Or in rain?
GROUP	Fire burn, and cauldron bubble!
VOICE 1	When the hurly burly's done, when
VOICE 2	The battle's lost and won.
VOICE 3	That will be ere the set of sun.
ALL	Double, double toil and trouble.

aha! Process, Inc.
(800) 424-9484

GROUP   … Broth boil!

ALL   Broth bubble!

Ongoing.
STORM   …

ALL   LIFE'S BUT A WALKING SHADOW …

GROUP   A POOR PLAYER … hand in hand,

VOICE 1   Posters of the sea and land

VOICE 2   Thus do go about …

VOICE 3   'Tis time! 'Tis time!

VOICE 2   … Thrice to thine

VOICE 3   And thrice to mine

VOICES
2 & 3   And thrice again to make up nine.

VOICE 1   Peace!
Pause. Listening.   PEACE!

All join STORM   Peace-s-s-s-s-s!
and make a hissing …

STORM   Sss …
… sound that
continues for
several seconds.

GROUP   Fire burn, and cauldron bubble,

VOICE 1   Cool it with a baboon's

VOICE 2   Blood … then

VOICE 3	The charm
VOICE 1	Is firm
VOICE 2	And
VOICE 3	Good.
ALL	Double, double toil and trouble!
STORM	…
GROUP	Heaven knows what she has done.
VOICE 2	By the pricking of my thumb
GROUP	A DRUM!
ALL	Something wicked this way comes!
GROUP	A POOR PLAYER THAT STRUTS AND FRETS HIS HOUR UPON THE STAGE
VOICE 1	AND
VOICE 2	THEN IS
VOICE 3	HEARD NO MORE.
GROUP	… A TALE
VOICE 1	TOLD BY AN IDIOT,
VOICE 2	FULL OF SOUND AND FURY,
VOICE 3	SIGNIFYING NOTHING!
GROUP	Heaven knows ...
ALL	What's done cannot be undone.

aha! Process, Inc.
(800) 424-9484

Woman's scream!

    GROUP   Good God, forgive us all!

Drum sounds.

    VOICE 1   A drum!

All this runs
together, echoing.

    GROUP   DR-rum!

    VOICE 2   A drum!

    GROUP   DR-rum!

    VOICE 3   Macbeth doth

    VOICE 3 &
    GROUP   Come!

    STORM   (Hissssssssssessss.)

Then screaming,
running wildly …
and … freezing.

Storm sounds get
louder, then softer,
then stop.

Blackout.

A Play in One Act
Izack, Einstein, and Lady M
Cheryl E. Davis

CHARACTERS

BERRY
[BERRY]   ... not a cool dresser

EDDIE
[EDY]   ... surfer dude, street or beach

FONSO
[ALLY]   ... cool, "the bomb" (to kids, not parents
                            or teachers)

ROXY
[ROCKY]   ... whatever ... Harley to hip hop

LUCY,
TYRA, &   ... cheerleaders
CHAREE

MICHAEL   ... jock, sometime Lucy boyfriend

P.A.   ... voices from a public-address speaker

OFFICER LARRY   ... school security officer

OTHER STUDENTS ... as needed to make up a classroom

MRS. VINGH   ... a substitute teacher, new to America;
                            a little difficulty with English but not
                            with students

aha! Process, Inc.
(800) 424-9484

THE SETTING

When the lights come up we see a very traditional American History classroom. Flags of the original 13 colonies, blue and gray battles on a large U.S. map, Lee and Grant and Appomattox posters.

The desks are in rows facing the back of the stage. Chalkboards, a hall door, and a teacher's desk are along the entire back of the stage.

Lights up!
There is no teacher.
Just students …
sitting, straddling,
and perched on desks,
mostly downstage,
talking to and arguing
with each other.

Girlz get mad, as
Fonso stands up
and then sits down.

        FONSO   Lady Macbeth hooked up the whole thing.

Boyz agree.
Girlz get angrier.

        ROXY   A'right. A'right. What do you mean "hooked up"?

        MICHAEL   She made it happen.

        EDDIE   Like, it was the **witches** who made it happen.

        BERRY   Omens!

        EDDIE   OK, o-mens made it happen.

        LUCY   They just started it.

aha! Process, Inc.
(800) 424-9484

FONSO
Loud agreement and disagreement.

I mean, his lady made Macbeth kill the king.

BERRY

And then kill Banquo and Macduff's whole entire family and anyone else he thought might get in his way?

Silence.
The boyz glare at him.
The girlz clap.

LUCY

OK, for once I agree with Berry, the Boy Wonder.

BERRY

I meant …

ROXY

Too late. We know what you meant.

FONSO
To Berry.

Thanks for backing me up.

EDDIE
To Berry.

Du-ude. Way to be on the wrong side.

Berry is embarrassed and sputtering, but no words come out.

BERRY

It's … just … well—it's true.

MICHAEL
He makes digging gestures, throwing the "dirt" on Berry. Then everyone—first the boyz, then even the girlz—pretends to throw dirt on Berry.

Stop now, Berry. Somebody take the shovel away from him.

*Other class members
come and stand
behind the action,
then go back when
it's over.*

Bell rings.
*Silence.
Everyone rearranges,
ending up the same.*

      EDDIE   Where's Gufferson? He's never late.
*They all repeat the
pretend dirt-throwing
and bury Eddie.*   Hey, I only meant ...
*Same show as before.
Same class movement.
Same rearranging and* OK. Now **I'm** sorry.
return to ... silence.

*Speaker on wall
comes on.
Everyone looks up.*

    P.A. SYSTEM This is Dr. Vesco.
*Class claps.
P.A. buzzes
on and off.*   That's enough. Is the sub in there?

    EVERYONE YES!

Silence.

      P.A.   This is Dr. Vesco.
Silence.   Ah ...
*Silence.
The buzzing on
and off continues.
Silence.*   This is Dr. Vesco.

Roxy and Lucy are motioning for everyone to be quiet. They are laughing but not making a sound.

This is Dr. Vesco.
Ah ...

There is muffled and squelching noise for a few seconds.

P.A.
A woman's voice.

Is your teacher there?

ALL
Controlling the laughter.

Yes.

Where is Dr. Vesco?

P.A.
Same voice.

Ah ...
Security is on its way. Let the sub speak.

Silence.

There is zero tolerance for this kind of behavior. **Where ... is ... the ... sub?**

ROXY
Yelling.

There ... is ... no ... sub!!

P.A.

The student who just said that: Identify yourself!

EVERYONE ELSE

THERE ... IS ... NO ... SUB!

P.A.

Identify yourself—now.

ALL
Say their own names all together.

!!!^&$$***()#$%^&*^$&*!!!!!

P.A.
Background CB
(Citizens Band) noise.   Larry ... Larry?
Muffled squelching.   What's your 20?

More CB noise.   Main hall, second floor.
Hard breathing.

Room G407 reports sub missing.   Copy?

Muffled.   Copy.

SECURITY
Bursting through
the door.   Copy!

CLASS   LAR-REE!   LAR-REE!!   LAR-REE!!!
Applauds.   Cop bows.

LARRY   OK, knock it off.

Class quiets.
To P.A. speaker—
and his radio.   No sub here.   Copy?
Class applauds again.

P.A.   Look—I mean, copy.   Look in the desk.
   Top right-hand drawer.

LARRY
Doing as directed.   I know the drill.   Copy.

P.A.   Left-hand side.   Should be a "Substitute" folder.
Lucy, Roxy, and
Fonso, who've been
listening, huddle
together, obviously
"hatching" some plan.

LARRY   Copy.
Reading.   "Substitute Lessons: Gufferson. Second Period."

P.A.	Find the "emergency" lesson sheet.

Berry joins the huddle.
They are hurriedly
talking, then writing
on a piece of paper.   I said, Find the—

LARRY	Copy.

P.A.	Now, find the "Class Assignment Section."

P.A. VOICES
Muffled.
In background, from
behind P.A. speaker,   You can use the radio now.
squelching feedback.

LARRY   Um ... looking, looking.
Going through every
drawer and piece
of paper.   Still—l-o-o-looking. Looking.
                   No. Not yet. No ...

Radio blares. He
secures his earpiece.
Getting very   I know. I know that. I am. Copy.
frustrated.   I AM reading what it says.
                    Still ... looking ...

The huddling group
un-huddles, and
Berry runs up and
puts a sheet of paper
in front of
Officer Larry.   Wait a minute ...
Berry pushes his
finger on the paper,
and Larry reads.   Yes, here it is. Class ... Assignment ... Section?

Looks at Berry.	
Berry nods (so do	
the others), and	OK, Class Assignment Section.
they get the class to	
nod, then look at	
the paper in front	
of Officer Larry.	Got it. Says: "Write Assignment on Board."
	I think it's a test.
Looks at kids.	
They all nod big-time.	
	Uh-huh. Got it.
Radio buzzes.	Copy.

P.A.	Officer Larry will be in your class until a sub is secured. Follow his directions as though he were your regular teacher. Mr. Gufferson and Dr. Vesco will be advised of your behavior choices.
Squelches off.	

All wait and then:
Silence.

CLASS	LAR-REE! LAR-REE!!
Clapping and cheering.	
FONSO	
To class.	COOL IT. **COOL** IT!
To Officer Larry.	Way to go, man!
They slap hands ...	
and then Fonso slaps	
with most of the rest	
of the class.	
LARRY	OK, OK. You said you have an assignment ... ABOUT HISTORY. Let's see, in particular—

Looks through papers he took out of the desk.	War-r-rr. Yup. War!
Sort of singing/saying and dancing the late-'60s song.	"War. Good grief: What is it **good** for? What is it **good** for?"
CLASS	Whoa … oo-o-o-a-ah!
LARRY *Ad-lib.*	"Absolutely nuthin'!"
CLASS *Clapping.*	Whoa-oo-oh-oo-oh-oo-ah!
LARRY *Bows. Clapping. Reading.*	Ah-hem! Thank you. Uh-huh!! OK, back to re-al-i-tee: In particular, **you** are supposed to be … getting ready for a big test about the similarities and differences between the Revolutionary and Civil wars?
Reading.	With dates … Dang! This is as hard as the citizenship test over at the federal building. So go ahead … give me that assignment you told me you had.
Pause.	One of you write it on the board.
Nobody moves.	There **has** to be an assignment on the board, and you have to be doing it before a sub gets in here, or we are in **big trouble**! And TROUBLE IS NOT ALLOWED ON MY WATCH!! So I'll be humming the *Jeopardy!* tune while you, especially you …
Pointing at the Berry group.	Yes. You. Look at me. Good. You too, Fonso. I'll give you time to come up with a spang-diddly-wowser, class-kickin', hard-workin', war-rippin', test-passin' assignment.
No one moves.	(Humming.) Move. Move, move.

The Berry group huddles again.   (Humming.)

The rest of the class gets restless and talkative. They look at each other until they look back at Larry and follow directions.   And the rest of you ...

    Hum along with me.

A couple of students mumble how stupid this all is.   I can't HEAR ... **ALL** of you!

Points at two boys who are making fun of everyone.   Drop and give me 20.

They do.   AND keep humming.
    I can't **hear** you ...

It gets louder. Counts with boys but repeats "19" about six times. Humming slows. Then stops. Silence.   OK, ladies and gentlemen! This is the moment. Will it be ... copy pages 167 to 170 and 211 to 215 (yes, I just found the **real** assignment)—**or** ... will the world-famous "Berry and the Sidekicks" provide us with their promised assignment?

Fingers extended, he does a drum roll on the desk as Lucy and Roxy head for the chalkboard.   Ladies ...

He bows and hands them chalk.   Pour lay youz!

LUCY   We

ROXY	Are NOT
BOTH *Finishing together …*	Berry's sidekicks!
LARRY *They nod and laugh.*	My mistake. Can you ever forgive me? I knew you could. Go on now. Time is money.
ROXY *She and Lucy and the rest slap hands. Larry looks doubtful.*	Actually, time is **space**! For real. Ask Mr. Donatelli.
LARRY	I … did not **know** that.
LUCY *Class mumbles.*	OK … First, I'm going to explain what we want to do and how we want to do it … to everyone, and then Roxy will write it on the board, and then we'll do it. OK. OK. We're, like, going to do an improvisation and go back in time to the Revolting—
BERRY	Revolutionary.
LUCY	Whatever! … Revolutionary War and then to the Civil War, which we all know about, but not as much as the Revolutionary one because Mel Gibson's son in "The Patriot" was like—
TYRA & CHAREE	So-o-oo cute!
CLASS MEMBER 1	What's an improv-erd-sation?
ROXY	Improvisation. Improv. You know, scenes you make up and act out. Without a script: just from ideas and situations.

SEVERAL CLASS MEMBERS	We don't get it. Besides, this is too corny, man.
ROXY *Writing as she talks.*	Look! No. 1. We make a timeline of both wars; we copy it
FONSO	Together—on pages 170 and 215.
ROXY	Then we make a list of facts for each war.
EDDIE	Then, dudes, we pick people to **be** from one or the other war.
BERRY	People who really existed.
LUCY	We don't make up that part.
TYRA	And list facts about that person. So we know about them. And decide stuff about them … well, because we're pretending to **be** them.
ROXY	No. 2. Pick a person.
CHAREE	So we can act like them. Or is it **talk** like them?
FONSO, EDDIE, & BERRY	Both.
LUCY	Then …
ROXY	No. 3.
LUCY	We're going to create a moment and bring them together and let, like, the first Americans from our first wars **talk** to each other.

TYRA	How many wars have we had? I thought War One and War Two were all, except for the one in V-v-v? No. Nam? Yeah, NAM.
ROXY	VIET Nam. It's WORLD War One and WORLD War Two. And Korea. My grandpa says everyone forgets that one.
TYRA	MY dad calls that other one NAM!
CHAREE	So does my Uncle Wally.
BERRY	Short for Viet—
ROXY	Nam.
LUCY	HEL-LO? Could we get back on the subject? We're going to bring together people from the Revolutionary War of 1776 and the War of 1812.
CHAREE	1860.
BERRY	1861 to 1865.

Lucy gives them The Hand. (Holds up her hand to them and looks away.)

CLASS MEMBER 1	Bring together? Like, this is too weird.
EDDIE	Exactly, dudes and dudettes! Weird Improvisational Theatre. We'll take this, like, imaginary ride and put people from different times together. Yes-s!
FONSO	And see what happens.
BERRY	Think of it as a MIND time machine.

aha! Process, Inc.
(800) 424-9484

Sarcastically.

**CLASS
MEMBER 1** A "Kodak Moment" in a History class?!

Grumbling.

**SEVERAL
CLASS
MEMBERS** This doesn't make any sense. **And** it's stupid.

Ad-lib with others.

EDDIE "PlayStation," man.

ROXY Without the wires.

FONSO Hooked up with "Whose Line Is It Anyway?"

**CLASS
MEMBER 1** You can stop selling now. AND I still don't get it.

ROXY
Stepping toward "1." Get out of your Lizard Brain and **get this**!

**CLASS
MEMBER 1** Did she just call me a lizard?
Others laugh.

**ROXY,
LUCY,
CHAREE,
& TYRA** If the breath FITS ...

*Stepping between
them.*
BERRY How about ... we'll just show you a little
demonstration of what we're talking about.

*Turning toward Roxy
and walking away
as he talks to her.* Pick someone you know about.

ROXY Lady Macbeth!

BERRY No, someone REAL.

ROXY She's as REAL to me as **you** are.

The others step up.
Eddie walks Berry
away from Roxy
until she and Berry
are separated.

BERRY OK, someone **REAL** that you've been studying in **school** or in a **book.**

Separately at first.
Then finishing
together. Backing
Berry up as they go.
Pretending to read
from a book.

ROXY Yet, Macbeth, I do fear thy nature.

The other girls
pantomime reading
from books.

LUCY It is too full of the milk of human kindness

CHAREE To catch the nearest way

ROXY Hurry hither,

TYRA That I may pour my spirits in thine ear;

LUCY And chastise ... with my tongue—

ROXY —**From** the play **written** by William Shakespeare **studied** in a class **taught** by Mr. Donatelli, in this very school—"And chastise ... with my tongue—"

**CLASS
MEMBER 1** Wait. Wait. What the heck are you **talking** about? It sounds like English. But it ain't English to me.

Roxy snaps at Lucy.

ROXY Translation girl?

LUCY Yes?
Playing along.

ROXY He needs his Shakespeare explained.

"Valley speak" or Brooklyn accent. Chewing pretend gum.

LUCY Don't we all. 'K.
Dude named Macbeth gets visited by a seer who says that he'll be all that, including the king—who, by the way, is very healthy and staying with the Macbeths at that particular moment.

Macbeth's wife has just found all this out from a letter he wrote to her. Now she's worried Macbeth ain't man enough to kill the king and win the kingdom. Oh, it's not modern times where murder was so much against the law if you were a king.

ALL All that impedes thee from the golden crown! … Come, thick night … so my sharp knife see not the wound it makes …

ROXY Nor heaven peep through the blanket of
They all turn away the dark to cry …
from the others.

Pause.

aha! Process, Inc.
(800) 424-9484

Turning in unison.

ALL   Stop! Stop!

Pause.
They turn back and
quickly turn around
together as The
Supremes and
start singing.   OO-OOO-OO—
"SSSS-Stop. In the name of love.
Before you break my heart, think it o-o-ver!"

Class applauds.

FONSO   Give it up. You pick someone, Berry.

BERRY   Sir Isaac Newton. Scientist—**real** person.
He formulated the Laws of Physics ... well,
most of them. And made science the way it is
today.

TYRA   Who?

CHAREE   Fig Newton.

To the others.

LUCY   No fig. Isaac Newton.

TYRA   Who you picked, because he was a general in
the Civil War ...?

BERRY   No. Because Sir Isaac Newton figured gravity
out, among other things.

LUCY   Which war?

FONSO   Looks like the Civil War.
Sarcastically.   Good choice, Berry. Fits right in with Lady M.
Also a famous Civil War general.

TYRA   Oh, Newton, the apple-dropping-on-the-head
guy.

BERRY	He was born the year Galileo died: 1642.
CHAREE	For real? Berry picks a 400-year-old guy. FOR REAL.
ROXY	OK, now that we have a for-real someone, someone else pick someone. C'mon.
Silence.	Fonso? Eddie? Lucy?

EDDIE
Pushes his hair out. **Speaks with a German accent.** *Clicks his heels together.*

Einstein. Dr. Albert Einstein.

Ya! Herr Einstein.

At your service! Also **totally** nothing to do with the Civil War. But I know a lot about him. And even though none of our characters is a real part of the Civil War, this is just a demo. We can pick people from that time when everyone gets it. OK?

FONSO	For now.
TYRA	How old's **your** guy?

Eddie looks at Berry, who whispers to Fonso.

FONSO	He died about 50 years ago. He invented the A-Bomb.
BERRY	Not really. His theories made it possible for the Atomic Bomb to be invented.
CLASS MEMBER 1	He's the old science guy with the freaky hair and big mustache.

MICHAEL   Who chooses Pepsi over Coke. A no-brainer!

EDDIE
Hand-slapping.   When he should just do the Dew!

LUCY
Going to the
chalkboard
with Fonso.   OK. We need at least 10 facts about the Civil
War. I'll write.

LARRY   For those of you new to this, the textbook has a
very complete summary of Civil War facts,
right along with the time line—

FONSO   On page 215.

There is a sudden
storm of students
and backpacks and
books and notebooks
and getting them open.

LUCY   OK. Go!

She writes down
the words that are
in ***bold face.***

*****NOTE************************
The following lines,
or parts of lines, are
the facts. Some
facts may be more
important personally
to some students. It
is the clear intention
of the author and
publisher that these
lines/facts be as

aha! Process, Inc.
(800) 424-9484

evenly and randomly
divided up among the
readers/actors as
possible to avoid
having any fact or
historical conclusion
being identified with
any one character.
In order to emphasize
the importance of
fact-based opinions,
the following activity
is suggested.

[After the second
reading, all readers
or reader groups
need to verify these
facts and have their
own sources to
support what
they say.]

****

FACT 1	The **first shot** of the war was fired at Fort Summer by the South in South Carolina.
FACT 2	SumTER. Fort **Sumter!**
FACT 3	The South had the cute **gray** uniforms.
FACT 4	Because the Union already used the **blue** ones.
FACT 5	The war was about **slavery.**
FACT 6	The North was **against** it.
FACT 7	The South was **for** it.

FACT 8   Yeah, but everyone says the war was about who had **more power** over states, the **federal** government or each **state.**

FACT 9   Well, the North thought **slavery was wrong,** even if at that time it was legal.

FACT 10   The North, the Union, was called **THE YANKEES.**

FACT 11   The North wanted everyone to stay in the Union—stay together as the **United States.**

FACT 12   The South was called the Confederacy, THE **REBELS.** They wanted out, to make their own separate country—the Confederate States of America.

FACT 13   The Northern states **abolished** slavery. Made it illegal.

FACT 14   The Southern states, like the Southern colonies, made it legal to own slaves. And illegal to help them escape. **Slave labor** kept the South in business, and that business kept the North's factories going.

Lucy stops writing because she can't keep up.

FACT 15   Many Northern states argued for the abolition of slavery even during the writing of the Declaration of Independence and the Constitution. But those states did not have enough votes and had to compromise. The South blocked what many in the North wanted to do.

FACT 16	A hundred years later, with more states added to the Union, the North had the votes to change the law, so the South wanted to be left alone, or they wanted **out of the Union.** And the North wanted to stop that from happening.
LUCY	That's **WAY** 10! Including all the things that were said at least **50 times.**

**CLASS
MEMBER 1**
Sarcastically.   OK. Now what? I want to see how the three space cadets get together in that **MIND** travel machine so we can have this precious moment you've been talking about.

Ignoring the attitude.

FONSO	We still need a couple of more things—for the improvisation to work.
ROXY	We need a setting.

The same class members who don't like this activity show they still don't.

EDDIE	You know, the set—where the action is.
LUCY	The stage.
TYRA	Conflict.

**CLASS
MEMBER 1** They have a war, don't they?

Laughter.

BERRY	Good point.

aha! Process, Inc.
(800) 424-9484

Almost sincerely.

CLASS MEMBER 1   Thanks.

CHAREE   They could be against war and **for** killing. Like capital punishment.

The class is stunned and silent momentarily.

ROXY   I can't believe you just said that.

CHAREE   Me neither. Sorry.

FONSO   No, it was good.

ROXY   Extremely! I'm not being sarcastic either.

BERRY   Einstein was a pacifist. He was against war.

MICHAEL   The bomb guy?

EDDIE   Yes. What about Newton?

BERRY   I just know he was grumpy. And not very outgoing. He even kept his discoveries to himself.

FONSO   Another "Brain in a Box"?

BERRY   Possibly.

ROXY   Lady Macbeth was definitely **for war.**

FONSO   OK. Conflict. Characters. Civil War with facts … a personal position for each of them … We still need an action situation, a set.

TYRA   McDonald's.

CHAREE	An elevator.
LUCY	The mall.
MICHAEL	A basketball game.
ROXY	The Oscars.
BERRY	Sightseeing. No, that's lame, even to me.
EDDIE	A party!
CLASS MEMBER 1 *Finally interested.*	A RAVE, man. An all-nighter. Your parents think you're on a Scout trip.
EDDIE	And the ravers are wearing only blue or
TYRA	Gray.
LUCY	And fights are breaking out all over. And gray and blue are such sucky colors.
CHAREE	Purple and yellow.
TYRA & EDDIE	Yes-s-s! They can be wearing either purple or yellow!
FONSO	Suddenly a sunspot sets off a series of warps in space—
LARRY	And time. Go on; keep going.
EDDIE	A warp in space and time that collides and interrupts these three lives—
LUCY	Lady Macbeth didn't actually have a real life.

ROXY	Well, she did, but Shakespeare basically made her up. He can just come from his time as Lady Macbeth. Serves him right too for not letting women play ladies' parts.
EDDIE	And the warp drops them all into this big rave party called "The American Civil War."
ALL	A'r-IGHT!
ROXY	OK, OK. Seems like we're still missing something.

Cynically.

CLASS MEMBER 1	Yeah, like what is the **reason** for doing this whole big history party improvisation thing?

The eight react happily.

LUCY	Give Mr. Bad Attitude a hand.

They all clap. The class member falls out of his chair.

Stepping back to help the guy get up.

FONSO	You're the bomb, man.
ROXY	We need to know Gufferson's question.

LUCY
To Officer Larry.

	We need the essay question about the Civil War.
LARRY	Actually, Berry gave me two questions, and one is about the Civil War, and it's kinda like Gufferson's—except it's easier to figure out.
FONSO	Read.

TYRA	I thought we were doing an improv?
LUCY	We are. But Mr. Bad Attitude over there actually made a good point. The improvisation needs to answer the question we'll be asked.
CHAREE	OK …
TYRA	And that would be …?
ROXY *Sincerely.*	Let's hear the question first. Please?

To Roxy, then the other girlz.

FONSO	You said … **Please**? Officer Larry, read the question, *please*?!
EDDIE	And **please** hurry.
BERRY	Pretty **please.**
LARRY *Clears his throat.*	I'd— be **pleased** to.
LUCY	Stop anytime now.
CLASS *Laughter until Larry starts reading.*	*Please?*

LARRY	"What are the reasons that justify and fail to justify going to war against the English in 1776 and going to war against … ourselves … in 1861?"
LUCY	We'll use: "What are the reasons that justify and fail to justify going to war against ourselves in 1861?"

FONSO	OK, Berry, **PLEASE** 'splain that to us.
BERRY	Well, it's asking: What is the value of organizing a conflict into armies and fighting and killing until there is loser and a winner? Is the tension created socially from ... what I mean is ... will the result hold the society closer together or force a change, a break, in the society or societies involved in the conflict? And is that worth the cost to both sides? And is it inevitable that whomever—
LARRY	WHO-ever.
BERRY *Embarrassed.*	Excuse me ... Is it inevitable that WHOever wins that conflict gets unequal power at the expense of the side that loses?
Silence.	
EDDIE	I feel so ... so stupid.
ROXY	You'll get over it.
LUCY	Berry, relax. Now please explain it to us in English.
BERRY	I DID!
FONSO	Take it to the street, Berry.
ROXY	Oh, yeah. Bring it down—
EDDIE	Like wa-aay down, du-ude!
LUCY, TYRA, & CHAREE	Go Berry, go Berry, go—

BERRY | I don't know if I can. Besides Gufferson's going to put this question on the test, and it's going to be written pretty much the way I just said it.

EDDIE with CLASS MEMBER 1 This is a fact!

Total silence.

LARRY | Want some help?
Silence.

I can't hear you.

Not very enthusiastically.
ALL | Yes-s.

Sarcastically.
ROXY | Oh, yes. Yes, please, Officer Larry, please help us.

LARRY | Here's the long and short of the question as I happen to see it from my **lowly angle** here on the floor of all jobs: You got these two wars, almost a hundred years apart. Everyone do the math.

He waits.

All the colonists, north ones and south ones, don't like how the British are running things, so they revolt, **together**, and POINT: We **get** America.

Thirteen colonies become states of one government, these United States. And 100 years later add a few more states. And the states south of the Mason-Dixon line, somewhere south of Kentucky, don't like how the majority of states north of that line are always running things, so they try to pull out of the United States and start their own country. But they lose. POINT: We **keep** the United States of America.

Here's your question as I see it, no matter how fancy Mr. Gufferson and the textbook write it: What is the good news and ... and ... what is the BAD news about the Civil War?

Writing as she speaks.

ROXY   What is good ... and bad ... about the Civil ... War?

Sincerely.   This works.
Applause!
Getting control.

LUCY   OK, like I was saying—

ROXY   We really need the loud music ... and a drum roll!

FONSO   Pretend to hear it!

Roxy, Berry, and Eddie (who is combing his hair) push the   You guys ready? chairs out and put their backs to everyone—and freeze.   On three, two, one: It's SHOWtime!

Eddie turns suddenly. Using German accent.   Whoo-oop! Whoo-oop! Put your hands together. Let's hear it for da var!!

To the class members.   C'mon!
Gets them clapping to a beat.

CLASS
Answers him.   Whoo-oop! Whoo-oop!

EINSTEIN	Is da Eastside in da house?
CLASS	Whoop!
EINSTEIN	Der 'burbs?
CLASS	Whoo-oo-oop!
EINSTEIN	Der Southside Webels?
CLASS *Class gives a* *Rebel yell.*	Whoo-oo-oop!
EINSTEIN	Der North?
CLASS	Whoo-oo-oop!
EINSTEIN	I said, Is da North … I said, Is da Blue … Is da North and da Blue in da house?
IZACK *With a British accent.* *Turning around and* *going into character.* *Clapping stops.*	Excuse me, old boy. Just who are yelling at? And could you hold this racket down a bit?
EINSTEIN	Just who are you calling OLD? And dis isn't a racket, dis is a var. It says so on dis card.
IZACK	A var? I mean … war?
EINSTEIN	Unfortunately.
IZACK	Whose?
EINSTEIN	Vell, dat is a goot question. Da other goot question is, Who are you?

IZACK *They shake hands.*	I am Sir Isaac Newton, at your service. And may I ask, who are you?
EINSTEIN	Vell, I used to be Dr. Albert Einstein. But dis noise, dis place, gives me no clues about who else I could be, so all things being "w'elative" I am p'wobably still Albert Einstein, at your service. Und you can call me Al.
IZACK	Heavens no. That would be too familiar. I will call you Dr. Einstein.
EINSTEIN	Hmm. Den I vill call you Zack. You der, Mr. I-Zack Newton boy …
IZACK *In thick British accent.*	I say. This is highly irregular. You a very preposterous person, and this is a very illogical situation.
EINSTEIN	No, yes, donk-uh-shane, I am. But dis situation is logical. I can assure you of dat. It is just dat we have not yet figured out der logic!
IZACK	I have a mind to agree with you, sir.
Screaming and running at Izack and Einstein. **LADY M**	Aaaaaahhhhh!!!!
They scatter, regroup, then scatter again.	AAAAAAAAAHHHHH!
EINSTEIN *Putting his hand over her mouth. She keeps screaming, but it's muffled.*	Hello der!

LADY M	Aaaaaahhhhh.
To both of them.	Identify yourself.
Silence.	Are you Blue or Gray?
Interrupting from the audience.	
LUCY	Purple or Yellow!
Roxy waves her away.	
LADY M	I am see-eeing another color …
IZACK	No you're not—
To Lucy.	You can't change the colors. It's a historical fact.
Short staring contest. Berry wins.	
LADY M	Again I ask you, each of you, which side are you on, the Blue or the Gray?
EINSTEIN	Blue und Gray? Dis all has a familiar ring to it.
IZACK	How? And my dear mistress, please be more respectful of your elders and stop that dreadful screaming. And do not assume we know anything about this circumstance, especially not a war. And blue and gray are NOT familiar colors representing anything to me.
LADY M	That's because you're too old. Besides, you are in a time warp.
IZACK	Mathematically impossible.
EINSTEIN	Vell, in your time, you are very correct. But by my time in the 19th and 20th centuries der are some mathematical theories and discoveries dat make time and space, vell, if you can travel at the speed of light, it makes a time varp interesting and possible, if not very p'wobable.

To Izack.

LADY M   You've been jumped ahead in time

To Einstein.   You've been jumped **back.**

EINSTEIN   Ah yes. De American Civil Var. The two opposing sides vore blue und gray.

IZACK   Back? Ahead? Where? Why? **America** is a little colony hardly worth the tobacco it brings to England. It has been a good place for Puritans. But Jamestown did not work out.

EINSTEIN   America isn't England's colony anymore.

IZACK   The Spanish rule then? No, not the **French**?

Einstein shakes his head.

EINSTEIN   No, da colonies are now da United States of America.

IZACK   By Jove.
To Lady M.   What is it, then, that you have brought me— us—to?

LADY M   Back, to answer some hard questions.

IZACK   Hardness is the mathematical result of the temperature of matter and the equality of the other forces pushing against each other.

LADY M   Hardness is also what happens when people want two opposite but equal things.

EINSTEIN   Ved-d-dy in-ter-esting. Den, da forces must somehow be **un**equalized.

IZACK	Raa-therr! But changing the force of one side may cause such inequality that the only result will be total destruction. I must say, though, that human forces do not lend themselves to mathematical exactness or equations.
LADY M *Starts screaming.* *They start running.*	Total destruction ... the spirit of war. That's me! Aaaaaahhhhhggghhh!
IZACK	Very well cast.
EINSTEIN *To Izack.*	Indeed. If dis machine could move you to my time, to Germany, you vould experience a spirit of var and bloody murder and horror equally unparalleled—though the technology of var vas far superior to the technology of dis Civil Var.
LADY M *Melodramatically.*	The Civil War was a bloody, bloody war too. When murder becomes the way to achieve what you want, the shedding of blood seems to continue and continue, like— these spots, these bloody spots that I wash and wash and cannot get clean from my hands or my soul.
IZACK	I daresay. What caused this Civil War of yours?
EINSTEIN	Forces once balanced und expressed in da form of speeches und votes vere exchanged for guns und armies.
IZACK	What did their king do?
LADY M	America elects its rulers, and they must stay inside certain laws in order to rule.
IZACK	Well, that is Revolutionary.

EINSTEIN Und vhat they can und cannot rule on are set. Dey are der legal, human, God-given rights protected in da Constitution.

IZACK Citizenship of humanity. No king. That is very radical ... quite a bold experiment. But I can not tell what brought this war on.

LADY M The balance was off from the beginning. The rights of citizenship were narrowly decided. Only men—and only white men—were considered full citizens, according to the Constitution.

IZACK Of course. They were ... Englishmen. They will take care of everyone else, like any good English gentlemen. Gentlemen, take over the kingdom. Hear, hear! Do you have royalty still with the landowners?

EINSTEIN Oh, no, da closest thing to royalty in America is movie—

LADY M And rock stars.

IZACK Do tell. This is not a planetary notion then?

EINSTEIN No.

LADY M Anyway, the country's founders could not resolve what to do with the Southern colonies who imported and bought and used slaves to produce cotton and other crops.

IZACK Indentured servants?

EINSTEIN No. Not servants who couldn't pay der debts.

LADY M People—men and women and children who were kidnapped from Africa and brought to America where they were sold as a commodity.

EINSTEIN	Bought und sold.

Getting into it.

LADY M	And I burned my lust for power into the hearts of those Southern gentlemen.
IZACK	Oh, dear.
EINSTEIN	I think Lady M here is just getting started.
LADY M	And I burned anger into the hearts of the Northern gentlemen so they would take offense and cease to negotiate—until all sides were plotting and trying to make people choose sides and make their own ambition more important than keeping a nation together **until** a fight, hand to hand, blow by blow, musket to musket, brother to brother, sword to sword—
EINSTEIN	Enough. Enough alw'eady.
IZACK	I think a king would have been very helpful here.
LADY M	Abe Lincoln was the newly elected president of the United States. And he was from the North. And he knew if he gave in and let the South go, there would be no war—but also no way to keep the king and the English from trying all over again to get back "their" colonies.
IZACK	So he had to fight back.
EINSTEIN	Da energy und force of da Southern Confederacy required an equal und opposite force in return. Zack, I believe you wrote somevhat on da subject of force und motion.
IZACK	Ah, yes, in physics, my Third Law of Motion.

EINSTEIN	I dhink your first Law of Inertia represents da initial issue dat set this var off.
LADY M	Really? I thought it would be the spirit of murder and taking power.
IZACK	Your murderous power is the force it takes to push the "inertia," so to speak, of making slavery in a land of freedom finally illegal. What does the M stand for?
EINSTEIN	Un Lady Macbeth.
IZACK	**Shake**speare's Lady Macbeth?
LADY M	Da von und only!
IZACK	Egads, truly a character that portrays the evil possible in the human desire for ambition.
EINSTEIN	She "hooked up" da whole murder of Duncan und all of Macbeth's villainy!!!

Boyz cheer!
Girlz boo!

IZACK	And rise to power. As did those witches!

Boyz cheer!
Girlz boo!

LADY M	But the murder was done by Macbeth—and even when his wife was sleepless and grieving over what she had done and had repented—but not Macbeth. Oh, no. He continued.
IZACK	Once something is in motion it tends to stay in motion unless some other force acts against it with an energy equal to the mass in motion.
EINSTEIN	Uh-huh. Vhat he said. Go Zack, go Zack.

Izack takes a bow.
Class applauds.

EINSTEIN   So. Da Civil War vas der only force big enough to move out da entrenched, inert, and inhumane force of slavery in America?

IZACK   Ah, I did not say only. It was, however, the force that was used.

The P.A. speaker clicks and buzzes.

P.A.
Previous woman's voice.   Excuse me.
Pause.
Larry's CB squeaks and breaks up.   Is a teacher in there yet?

Several class members look up and start to say something ...
Larry motions for them to be still.

LARRY   No. The assigned teacher's NOT in here yet.

Momentary blackout.

Bell rings.
Lights up.

There are a lot of students leaving class and coming in, along with door closings, greetings, and desk shuffling. This could be created before and taped to be played here,

creating time to clear the area in front of the board with desks left and right.

When the lights come up we can see three distinct groups perched and sitting toward the open area ... talking intently with each other, but answering "HERE" as the substitute teacher, Mrs. Vingh, standing in the middle of the open area, finishes calling the roll. She puts the attendance sheet outside the door.

At the door.

MRS. VINGH OK. Let us finish the explanation of the Officer Larry's assignment.

BERRY Actually, none of us is as good at explaining it as just doing it.

MRS. VINGH This is very interesting.

LUCY The board says it all.

ROXY Really.

EDDIE Like, not exactly. At least I've never **heard** the board talk.

Class breaks up laughing, including Mrs. Vingh.

aha! Process, Inc.
(800) 424-9484

MRS. VINGH   I am very glad for that.

LUCY   He knows what I meant.

MRS. VINGH   I am knowing too. Perhaps in several years technology will have talking boards. OK. You will show me how this assignment …

Reading.   "The GOOD and BAD of the American Revolutionary and Civil Wars" will be working today.

ROXY   And tomorrow and the next day.

FONSO   There are three presentations.

BERRY   Why did you call it the "American" … wars?

LUCY   Chill out, Berry.

ROXY   He didn't mean anything by that.

MRS. VINGH   Oh, I am very chilled out myself. It's just that almost every country has a revolutionary war or two. And very few countries exist for very long without experiencing a civil war. I have to remember this is **American** History so I don't mix up facts from any other revolution— or civil wars. Good question … Thank you, Mr., ah—

She looks at a class list. Reading …   Ah, Mr. Raspberry B. Johnson.

*The class **cracks up.** Except the Science study group and Mrs. Vingh. Fonso stops the laughing by standing up.*   Oh my … This is not my intention.

FONSO   It's a typo, Miss. It happens a lot.
To class.

His name is Berry.

CLASS   Hey, s'u-up, Berry?
Fonso sits.

MRS. VINGH Then, my mistake. How do you say it?
Oh yes. "MY BAD," Berry.
Class applauds.   OK, now, let's get this class on the road.

Blackout.

aha! Process, Inc.
P.O. Box 727
Highlands, Texas 77562
(800) 424-9484
fax: (281) 426-5600

www.ahaprocess.com

Want your own copies? Would you like to give a copy to a friend?

Please send me:

_____ Copy/copies of *Berrytales*

Books: 1-4 books $25/each+$4.50 first book plus
                                       $2.00 each additional book
                                       shipping/handling
             5 or more $20/each + 8%
                                       shipping/handling

Mail to:

Name: _____
Organization: _____
Address: _____

_____
Phone: _____ Email: _____

Method of Payment:
PO # _____
Credit card type: _____ Exp: _____
Credit card number: _____
Check: $ _____ Check # _____

Subtotal: $ _____
Shipping: $ _____
Sales tax: $ _____ (7.75% in Texas)
Total: $_____